The Journal of the
Hannah Arendt Center for
Politics and Humanities
at Bard College

The Journal of the Hannah Arendt Center for
Politics and Humanities at Bard College

hac.bard.edu

Published by
The Hannah Arendt Center for Politics and Humanities at Bard College
Roger Berkowitz, Editor
Tara Needham, Managing Editor

Produced by
Bard College Publications Office
Mary Smith, Director
Ann Forbes Cooper, Copy Editor
Karen Spencer, Designer

ISSN: 2168-6572
ISBN: 978-1-936192-74-8
Bard College, PO Box 5000
Annandale-on-Hudson, NY 12504-5000
bard.edu

Foreword

Thinking and action inform each other. The liberal idea that all people are equal or at least that they should be equal in a political way, has changed the world. So too has the Marxian thought that equality should extend to material as well as political relations. And action, like Martin Luther King Jr.'s "I Have a Dream" speech alongside the Civil Rights Movement has changed the way people think. But thought and action can also cancel each other out. Too much thought and one stands still, as does Socrates on his way to the Symposium. If one acts too much, there is no time to think: "Don't think, just do," as Tom Cruise intones in the latest *Top Gun*.

If one reads through Hannah Arendt's *Denktagebuch*, there are no more common entries than those titled some version of "Thinking-Acting." Thinking—the two-in-one dialogue with oneself in solitude—and action—the meaningful insertion of oneself into the common world—are the two polarities of Arendt's work. Arendt was a thinker of action, but one who acted, only rarely, at those moments of crisis. How then should a center dedicated to nurturing the spirit of Arendt's political thinking navigate the Scylla and Charybdis of unworldly thought and overly-worldly action?

The tension between action and thought has inspired the Hannah Arendt Center since its first conference, Thinking in Dark Times: Hannah Arendt's Ethical and Political Thinking. We have largely tilted the scales to the side of thinking, insisting that thinking about our world is an essential way to impact and change the way we live together. We have often been asked—sometimes pushed and cajoled—to have our conferences end with position papers or policy proposals. We have resisted what my friend Austin Sarat calls "the pull of the policy audience." Thinking frees one from conventions, ideologies, and habits. It is in the practice of thinking freely inspired by literature, philosophy, history, and art that we can be inspired to rethink and reimagine the political questions of our time.

Our 2021 conference Revitalizing Democracy: Sortition, Citizen Power, and Spaces of Freedom—the transcripts from which form the majority of this volume—came closer to embracing political action than ever before. There is an argument in many of these talks now turned into essays that randomly selected citizen assemblies might be a partial cure for the collapse of our sclerotic, technocratic, and elite-driven politics. Some believe that citizen assemblies lead to better and more just policies. Others, like myself, focus on the power of citizen assemblies to turn citizens away from private interests and towards the public interest. In both cases, there is a hope that citizen assemblies might be a remedy for our democratic crisis. And this July at Bard College the Arendt Center will host a workshop training nearly 40 government officials in the United States on how to employ citizen assemblies in their jurisdictions.

At the same time, these essays approach the question of citizen assemblies from an intellectual and humanist perspective. The effort is to think about the republican tradition of self-government, something that Arendt understood was not the same as democracy. These essays are more hopeful than much of what we publish. That too fit with Arendt, who always reminds us that we have the freedom and the power to think and act differently.

This volume of the *Hannah Arendt Journal* is dedicated to Tracy Strong who passed away in May 2022. Tracy was not only a brilliant political theorist and friend, he was also a huge supporter of the Arendt Center and participant in many Center events. Tracy spoke at our second conference Burden of Our Times as well as at our conferences Human Being in an Inhuman Age; Does the President Matter?; Hannah Arendt's *Denktagebuch*; and Revitalizing Democracy: Sortition, Citizen Power, and Spaces of Freedom. His talk at the 2021 Arendt Center conference is published in this volume of the *Journal* as, "Learning our Native Tongue: America as a Project."

—Roger Berkowitz

About the Hannah Arendt Center

Inspired by the spirit of Hannah Arendt, the leading thinker of politics and active citizenship in the modern era, the Hannah Arendt Center for Politics and Humanities at Bard College is the world's most expansive home for bold and risky humanities thinking about our political world.

The Hannah Arendt Center cares for and makes available nearly 5,000 books from Arendt's personal library, many with marginalia and notes. The Center oversees a variety of programs—the Courage to Be, Campus Plurality Forum, Race and Revolution, Bard Institute for the Revival of Democracy through Sortition, and Virtual Reading Group, among others—that combine courses, lectures, workshops, and symposia to bring Arendt's fearless way of thinking to a broad audience. The Center hosts lectures and special events on Hannah Arendt and relevant topics, all leading up to the annual fall conference, where philosophers, thinkers, and activists come together at Bard College's Annandale campus to discuss contemporary issues.

The Hannah Arendt Center hosts postdoctoral fellows, visiting scholars, senior fellows, and doctoral fellows who together contribute to the vibrant and engaged intellectual community at Bard College. Fellows teach one course per semester while pursuing their research. Thea Center's primary recurring fellowship is the Klemens von Klemperer Post-Doctoral Fellowship, a one-year teaching fellowship at the Arendt Center. Hannah Arendt Center produces several publications, including the weekly newsletter *Amor Mundi*, annual journal *HA*, and podcast *HAC*.

In 2020, the Center launched the Hannah Arendt Humanities Network (HAHN), which unites the institutions affiliated with the Open Society University Network to nurture a culture that values and strengthens the humanities as the foundation of an open society. HAHN hosts the Yehuda Elkana Fellowship and Prize (awarded to Uday Mehta in 2002), Network Faculty Seminars, a text seminar on Hannah Arendt's *The Human Condition* and *Vita Activa*, Artificial Intelligence Working Groups, Biannual Humanities Writing Retreats, and Bard High School Early College Network Course.

Above all, the Hannah Arendt Center provides an intellectual space for passionate, uncensored, nonpartisan thinking that reframes and deepens the fundamental questions facing our nation and our world.

VOLUME 10 *HA*

Revitalizing Democracy

Revitalizing Democracy: Sortition, Republicanism, and Citizen Power

Roger Berkowitz

It is Hannah Arendt's 115th birthday today, so Happy Birthday to her.

The title of this year's Arendt Center conference is Revitalizing Democracy: Sortition, Citizen Power and Spaces of Freedom; the title and the conference are attempts to talk to the sortition community, the group of activists around the world who are seeking to revitalize democracy through randomly selected citizen assemblies; my hope is to open them to a broader conversation from within a related and yet different tradition. Much of the writing on sortition has come from Europe and has been influenced by European ideas and practices of democracy. We see this in the Habermasian justification for citizen assemblies as tools to reach better and more rational decisions. In this talk I want to suggest an alternate foundation for citizen assemblies, one grounded in the American tradition of civic republicanism.

Republicanism is a contested idea, but it has its roots in the Latin *respublica*, or public thing. Republicanism is the political form of government that elevates the public interest over the individuals and factions who might pursue their private interests. For Baron von Montesquieu, republican government is activated by the virtue of the citizens, their acknowledgment of a common public interest. It requires a small republic so that there can be a sense of shared civic virtue and common values.

Often misunderstood is the complicated relationship between republicanism and democracy. Both are imagined as forms of self-government. But if democracy is the rule of the people and thus subject to the tyranny of the majority, republicanism aims to limit the will of the majority through counter-majoritarian institutions that aim to purse a common and public interest. What I would like to suggest today is that given the republican aspiration to forge a common interest beyond private interests, citizen assemblies are better understood within the republican rather than the democratic tradition.

The emerging story told about sortition connects it to democracy. By sortition I simply mean the practice of picking representatives by lottery. This tradition started in Greece and was continued in the Roman and Italian city states. Nearly every political thinker in history who considered the matter, from Aristotle to Rousseau to Montesquieu, believed that the selection of political leaders by lottery was a property of democracies. In this regard, sortition was contrasted with election, which was thought to be the way aristocracies picked their representatives.

There is a very simple reason for why elections are aristocratic and lottery is democratic. If you vote, generally you'll vote for people who have the virtue, the money, the education, and the status so that they seem to be qualified. Elections lead to a certain elite being elected; and that is often the goal of representative government, to ensure that the elite will govern. Selecting representatives by lottery includes a wider and less elite class of citizens and thus is associated with the democratic will of the people.

This traditional identification of democracy with lottery lasted until the United States Constitution. The US Founding Fathers were suspicious of democracy. They were small "r" republicans who wanted self-government and liberty, but were determined to avoid the dangers of democracy, including mob rule, tyranny of the majority, and the election of demagogues. Thus, the founders embraced the aristocratic practices of elections, the Electoral College, federalism, and constitutional limitation. From the United States Constitution onwards, electoral representation somehow supplanted lottery as the way democracies selected their rulers. Sortition disappeared from the political stage and democracy by the full extent of the people was betrayed.

Today, the movement for sortition is seen to be against elections, an effort to bring back lottery and thus revitalize democracy. David Van Reybrouck's book *Against Elections*, has done more to popularize sortition than any other book. Van Reybrouck argues that elections are antidemocratic and should be replaced or at least supplemented by randomly selected citizens assemblies. I generally find this story persuasive. I think it's an important story. And yet I want to challenge parts of it.

Specifically, I want to question the all-too-easy association of civic assemblies with democracy. I've been teaching two courses this semester. One is a course, with one of our keynote speakers, the aforementioned David Van Reybrouck. David has been helping students design civic assemblies for three local towns. One of the things you learn is how much effort and science and intellectual rigor goes into picking who's going to be selected. How do we do these random selections? What's the structure? Who are the experts? These citizen assemblies may be chosen by lottery, but they are designed and run according to formulas created by people we might call elites. They use "stratified selection" to correct for discrimination in the random selection of representatives. They're not simply purely random and they're moderated with facilitators trained in fostering dialogue and reaching consensus.

We must understand that the citizen assembly movement is not a democratic movement in the sense of bringing back direct democracy. It's better understood as a movement to re-engage citizens in the active practice of self-government. And that movement to revitalize the active practice to self-government is not, I think, necessarily democratic; at least within the tradition of American democracy, the embrace of citizen assemblies is more accurately described as a return to the tradition of civic republicanism. I've been struck by the way in which citizen assemblies and the sortition movement in many ways can be understood to be attempts to resurrect many of the ideas the US Constitution sought to embody but failed to preserve and actualize over its 200-and-some-odd-year history.

And this brings me to the other course that I'm teaching this semester, Constitutional Law. Remember that the US Constitution is not a democracy. It is imagined as a federal constitutional representative republic. It is republican, not democratic. Republicanism, the idea that people should govern themselves in the public interest, means that power lies in the people. From the Latin *respublica*, republicanism is the political form that sets the public interest above private interest; it stands for self-government by the people in the people's interest. For Montesquieu and other political thinkers, the republican form of government depends on the virtue of the people to act in the public interest. He thought republicanism could only work in a small republic with homogeneous citizens who shared a common sense of virtue.

In a large and pluralist commercial republic such as the United States, there can be no assumption of shared virtue. That is the why the framers of the American Constitution sought to create a constitutional republic that would employ institutional restraints and incentives to enable republican self-government even without a common virtue amongst the citizenry. One such check is a written constitution that limits majority rule. Another is the separation of powers, which establishes competing powers. A third limit on democratic rule is federalism, which divides power spatially across the country. All of these are republican institutions insofar as they take self-interested, passionate people and try and give them incentives to subordinate their private interests to a larger common and public interest.

In turning to republicanism, the American founders sought to correct for and prevent what they saw as the evils of democracy while still trying to hold on to the republican tradition of self-government and empowerment of the people. In fact, the Federalists, who were the people who helped write the US Constitution, were scared of democracy. As James Madison wrote in Federalist X: "A pure democracy, by which I mean a society, consisting of a small number of citizens, who assemble and administer the government in person, can admit of no cure for the mischiefs of faction." Alexander Hamilton said much the same in Federalist IX, that it is impossible to read the history of the petty democratic republics of Greece and Italy without feeling sensations of horror and disgust at the state of perpetual vibration between the extremes of tyranny and anarchy.

The American founders didn't want a democracy. There was a fear of mob rule. There was a fear that democracy, as Montesquieu had said, requires virtuous citizens. Thus, our American founders began from the assumption that people weren't virtuous, that people were self-interested and passionate, and that democracies would lead to short term failures that would lead to demagoguery.

One of the ways they sought to cure the dangers of democracy was through republican representation. The idea was that elites would represent the people and thus mitigate their most passionate and self-interested impulses. It was important for them that the representatives chosen were elites; what is more, they wanted a large republic since then there would be enough well-qualified elites to be chosen to lead. And thus, as Madison writes in Federalist X, "the elective mode of obtaining rulers is the characteristic policy of Republican government." The founders believed elective representation would be advantageous because it would elect elites and help cure some of the evils they saw in democracy.

The greatest fear that they had was that people would divide into factions and one faction would come to dominate and tyrannize the rest. I mean, that's an obvious danger in a democracy. It happens. It's happening right now in democracies around the world. Traditionally, the main factions in society have been the rich and the poor. But there are always different factions. And the worry is that in a democratic country, one faction would take over and oppress the others.

The question the American framers confronted was, how do you stop the great evil of politics, the dangerous vice of faction? The obvious answers would be to restrict liberty, to govern by elites, and tell people what they have to do. But the founders wanted to do the seemingly impossible: to preserve liberty and control the emergence and passions of factions. As Madison famously wrote in Federalist X, "Liberty is to faction what air is to fire." As long as you're going to let people be free, you're going to have factions. Any effort to eliminate factions would necessitate an unwanted attack on liberty.

This reflects one of Hannah Arendt's fundamental insights into politics, that people are plural. As long as you let people have different viewpoints. People are going to have different viewpoints. You're not going to get rid of it. No amount of education, no amount of science is ever going to convince people to agree. Factions are part and parcel of free and pluralist society. I am constantly hearing friends and student and colleagues saying, if we just educated people, they would all agree to get a vaccine, wear a mask, be prochoice, or whatever it is you want them to agree on. It doesn't work. Factions exist. Any government that doesn't take that into account is going to deny a kind of human nature. It is going to have to infringe on people's liberty of thought and action.

What the Federalists said is, okay, you can't take away the causes of factions without destroying liberty. So instead of addressing the causes of faction, you have to limit its effects. There were two ways to mediate the effects of factions. The first was replace virtue, the fact that people were supposed to be virtuous in a small republic, with the embrace of a large and pluralist country. The idea is that if you extend the expanse and you take in a greater variety of citizens, parties and interests, you make it less probable that a majority of the whole will have a common motive to invade the rights of other citizens. Basically, you divide and conquer.

The second approach that the Federalists took for the solution of the effects of faction was federalism. As Madison writes in Federalist 51:

> There are but two methods of providing against this evil [of faction]: the one by creating a will in the community independent of the majority, that is, of the society itself; the other, by comprehending in the society so many separate descriptions of citizens as will render an unjust combination of a majority of the whole very improbable. . . . The second method will be exemplified in the Federal republic of the United States.

Madison's federalist solution to the evil of faction is to create so many different centers of power in a republic—for example, in the federal government we have the separation of powers among Congress, the Supreme Court, the House, the Senate, the president, and also administrative agencies; and beyond the separation of powers, the federalist principle creates power centers in the then 13 states as well as in countless counties, towns, and civic associations. The power of federalism is that you create so many different power sources that there is a multiplication of power and there's no one ring that rules them all (excuse the Tolkien reference). There are multiple rings of power, and since different people and plural institutions hold the different rings, different power structures exist. If one institution or center of government gains too much power, others can combine to oppose it. The likelihood you end up with tyranny is small.

For Hannah Arendt, the federalist principle of the distribution of power is based on a quintessentially American experience, what she calls the new American experience of power. (*On Revolution*, 165) It started with Puritans fleeing religious intolerance in England. These Puritans, before landing at Plymouth Rock, met to determine and write down a constitution of liberties and powers that would determine the government of the future colony. Arendt allows herself to be struck by the fact that these poor travelers took upon themselves the right and the power to govern themselves—"The really astounding fact in the whole story is that their obvious fear of one another was accompanied by the no less obvious confidence they had in their own power, granted and confirmed by no one and as yet unsupported by any means of violence, to combine themselves into a 'civil Body Politick.'" (*OR*, 166) This feeling of empowerment for self-government was, Arendt argues, the ground of a truly new experience of power.

Alongside the American experience of power was the American "discovery of the federal principle for the foundation of large republics." (*OR*, 167) Arendt called this federal principle the "greatest revolutionary innovation" in the United States Revolution. What the American Revolution and US Constitution actually did was to institutionalize the new American experience of federated powers as new form of republican government.

Arendt was not some starry-eyed "America first" booster. She revered the American experiment in republican government; yet she also came to believe that the American experiment failed. She traces the failure of the American experiment as a federalist republic to the loss of American institutions of local power, institutions that at once would nurture the spirit of self-government and the American experience of power. She writes: "The Failure of the founders to incorporate the township and the town-hall meeting into the Constitution, or rather their failure to find ways and means to transform them under radically changed circumstances, was understandable enough." This failure had profound consequences: "[Jefferson] knew, however dimly, that the Revolution, while it had given freedom to the people, had failed to provide a space where this freedom could be exercised."

For Arendt, "The failure of postrevolutionary thought to remember the revolutionary spirit and to understand it conceptually was preceded by the failure of the revolution to provide it with a lasting institution." In short, Arendt saw the failure of postrevolutionary thought to remember the revolutionary spirit and understand its foundation in power. Jefferson knew that the US Constitution had failed to provide a space where this freedom and power could be experienced and exercised.

The Constitution failed to establish freedom, the fundamental experience of American power— which was found in townships, in the fact that people got together and talked to one another and governed themselves on local levels. Because of this failure, the people withdrew from public action and the public spirit was diminished. Since the Constitution itself provided a public space only for the representatives of the people and not for the people themselves, it is not surprising that the people would retreat from public engagement into their private and social lives.

The real danger Arendt saw was that we would lose spaces of freedom, spaces of power where people could get together and talk. And so, she writes, the whole question of representation—the focus on electoral representation in lieu of popular self-government—actually implies no less than a decision on the very dignity of the political realm itself.

The argument I'm leading up to is that Madison, Hamilton, Jefferson and the founders innovated an idea of republican government distinct from mere democracy. They embraced representation but did so amidst the experience of local participatory self-rule; for this reason, they imagined the United States to be a republic and not a democracy. And it is in this context that Arendt saw representation as a problem. It is an affront to the dignity of the political realm because if you let representation replace people engaging in self-government, they will lose the dignity of being self-governing citizens.

What I'm trying to suggest here and what I think I'm hoping this conference and volume will begin to explore, is that I think civic assemblies are in many ways the lost space of republican freedom that Jefferson and Arendt so deeply valued. Citizen assemblies can be a new way to create institutional spaces for the people to engage in a dignified act of politics.

One model for this is the jury. Sometimes what we call civic assemblies are called civic juries. I like that term as an American political theorist because it speaks to the role of the jury, which we all here in the United States understand. I turn to Alexis de Tocqueville, who writes that "the jury serves to communicate the spirit of the judges to the minds of all citizens, and this spirit with the habits which attend to it is the soundest preparations for free institutions." (*Democracy in America*, 262)

If America failed to create a space for the people to discuss politics, it did create a space for people to discuss right and wrong the jury. The jury is an institutional space where Americans habitually come together to discuss what we should do in matters of right or wrong, who should be punished and who not. The jury inculcates the habit to engage in the spirit of judging outside of one's personal interest, of judging according to the public interest, according to the law, or what is right.

The great promise of citizen assemblies understood as republican institutions is that they can provide a space for people to gather together and engage in the spirit of public deliberation, of compromising and governing not according to one's personal interest. They can thus resist what Arendt calls "the crisis of representative government."

She says representative government is in crisis today, partly because it has lost in the course of time all institutions that permitted the citizens actual participation and partly because it is now gravely affected by the disease from which the party system suffers bureaucratized and the two parties tendency to represent nobody except the party machines.

It is in these new councils, these new citizen assemblies or civic juries, where we can find what Arendt calls the spaces of freedom. She writes, "The councils obviously were spaces of freedom. Councils where people came together and talked." Because when you talk, you express your viewpoint and people listen. It's called appearing in public. It's what makes you human for Hannah Arendt. And so, the issue at stake, she says, was representation versus action and participation. The councils were organs of action, the revolutionary parties were organs of representation.

What I'm trying to suggest, and what I'm hoping again will be fleshed out over the next two days, is that what we need to think of today is these citizen assemblies as part of a self-government tradition of citizen action of participation, a restoration and revival of the American republican tradition. That's not just American. That's happening around the world. We need to create new spaces of freedom.

References

Arendt, Hannah, *On Revolution* (First, Faber & Faber, 1963).

Tocqueville, Alexis de, et al, *Democracy in America* (Paperback ed., Univ. of Chicago Press, 2002).

Is it Too Late to Revitalize Democracy? Democratic Innovation on the Eve of Climate Collapse

David Van Reybrouck

Thank you, Roger, for these very kind words and for a fantastic introductory speech on the link between Hannah Arendt and Citizens' Assemblies. I would like to start with a number of observations.

Citizens' Assemblies on the Rise

Two weeks ago, 2,000 inhabitants of the City of Amsterdam found a letter on the doormat saying "Congratulations! You have been drafted by a lot for a Citizens' Assembly and you are invited to advise the City of Amsterdam on which extra measures should be taken to meet its climate objectives. Prior knowledge about the city or its climate targets is not required for participation."

First, in just two week's time, early November 2021, 100 of them will start their deliberations. They will learn from experts and each other, and at the end they will come up with a number of concrete policy recommendations. This will be Amsterdam's first formal citizens' assembly ever.

Secondly, yesterday, a citizens' panel of 50 Belgians was selected representing the country's diversity in terms of age, gender, level of education, and place of residence. From next week on, this group will discuss Belgium's role in the European Union and how that level of transnational governance can be democratized. This project is part of the Europe-wide Conference on the Future of Europe. It will be the very first formal citizens' assembly organized by the federal government of Belgium.

Thirdly, earlier this year, the German federal parliament held its first government-led citizens' assembly. One hundred and sixty-nine citizens from Germany came together to talk about Germany's role in the world and its foreign policy. And the Speaker of the House, 79-year-old Wolfgang Schäuble, a true veteran of German parliamentary democracy, said: "Everywhere in Europe and North America, where Western democracy exists, we are witnessing an increasingly weaker cohesion of the model. The connection between voters and those who are voted in has become weaker. We mustn't become a caste of our own. Rather, we should make a parliamentary democracy future-proof. . . . Citizens' assemblies can be an important step, not as an alternative, but as a reinforcement of parliamentary democracy."*** Now, these are pretty extraordinary words coming from such a senior figure in German politics. Schäuble is the longest-sitting Bundestag member in German history. He's been there since 1971. Meanwhile, at the local level in Germany, dozens of towns, cities, and municipalities have started organizing citizens' assemblies drafted by lot.

Fourthly, just half an hour ago, and I think you are the first audience in the United States to hear about it, the City Council of Paris has started voting on a bill enabling something even more daring, i.e., the establishment of a permanent citizens assembly with Parisians drafted by lot. It's almost too symbolic to be true. One of the most iconic cities in the world, the capital of the fifth-largest economy in the world, votes for a sortition-based Permanent Citizens' Assembly on the day Hannah Arendt was born.

Indeed, as Roger already said, Hannah Arendt would have turned 115 today, and I think she would have smiled seeing this upsurge of deliberative democracy. More than 70 years ago, she wrote a phenomenal text called *Introduction into Politics*. It's the most impressive text I've read since I arrived in the United States to lecture here at the Hannah Arendt Center more than a month ago.

Introduction into Politics

The text was written in the second half of the 1950s, and like most of her groundbreaking work of that decade, it was written in German. At the time, she was living in the United States, commuting between New York City and Kingston, across the river from Bard College. Her essay never got published during her lifetime and was first printed in Germany in 1993. An English translation only came out in 2005.[1] Some of the ideas she developed, however, were taken up in *On Revolution* (1963), the book that was just quoted by Roger.

Introduction into Politics was heavily conditioned by the historical context in which it was written. The Cold War arms race took a scary turn when the United States and Russia tested their first next-generation thermonuclear weapons in the early 1950s, thus enabling global annihilation. And the Russian invasion of Hungary in 1956 shocked the world. Yet, regardless of these references, Arendt's essay turned out to be a universal text about politics and a pretty phenomenal one at that, too.

Hannah Arendt never wrote about sortition herself, but all arguments for deliberative democracy are already in this early essay of hers. Knowledge on how lottery was used as a democratic instrument in ancient Athens was still poorly understood in the 1950s. It was only in the 1990s, thanks to the work of the Danish scholar Mogens Herman Hansen, that we first got a detailed understanding of how Athenian democracy functioned in practice.[2] At the time of Arendt's writing, there was only one academic monograph available on the topic, James W. Headlam's *Election by Lot at Athens* from 1891, a work not present in the historical library of Hannah Arendt at Bard College.

Despite her silence on sortition, *Introduction into Politics* can be seen as a pivotal text of what has become the movement for citizens' assemblies. First, the title already alludes to a rather active role for citizens. "Introduction" here is not meant as a manual of political science or a preliminary course on political theory, but should be understood in its most literal sense: that of "Einführung," of being "led" into another space or realm, of being introduced into a new sphere. The translation of *Einführung in die Politik* as "Introduction *into* politics," rather than "Introduction *to* politics," as one might have expected, is therefore a fortunate one. It evokes the German accusative, the motion of being led into a different realm, in this case the political sphere. Whoever is introduced *into* politics, is brought into the space of thinking and speaking politically and is invited to become a political actor themselves. The proposition "into" transforms the person into an citizen, the passive outsider into an active insider.

The word "action" is key here. It refers to a central aspect of the Arendtian notion of democracy. The active citizen does not just undergo, receive or absorb the policies that have been concocted, packaged and shipped from above, but is deeply involved with shaping these policies themselves, alongside with others, within a space that allows for civic exchange of arguments and debate. In the polis, decisions "were not decreed from on high but decided by people talking with and persuading one another."[3] Having witnessed the mindless and thoughtless embrace of the Nazi ideology in her native Germany, Arendt defined democracy as a political sphere into which people are introduced to become active, thinking, and engaging participants—the very opposite of the numb, bureaucratic thoughtlessness she would later qualify Eichmann with.

Back to the Greeks

Arendt called for a radical rethinking of what politics *meant* and in order to do so she had to go down the historical ladder of political philosophy, beyond Marx and Kant, beyond Christianity and the Roman Republic, beyond Aristotle and Plato, even beyond the words of thinkers in order to look at the acts of citizens. She descended into time to look at Athenian democracy and how it functioned in the 5th- and 4th-century BCE. Just like Martin Heidegger felt dissatisfied with the history of Western metaphysics and returned to the pre-Socratic traditions of thinking in order to address the question of Being, Arendt felt disappointed with most political philosophy and felt the need to descend into the abyss of deep Greek time to look for the true meaning of politics: "The question about the meaning of politics (. . .) has hardly ever been asked in earnest since classical Antiquity."[4]

Disappointed by most political philosophy, she held that even the greatest philosophers were often surprisingly weak when it came to political philosophy. The reason for this? "The degradation of politics at the hands of philosophy, familiar since the days of Plato and Aristotle, depends entirely on the separation of the many from the few."[5]

This was a highly original thought. Trying to define politics was not about identifying individual or institutional features (like Plato, Aristotle, Hobbes, and Rousseau had been doing), but about something much more basic: recognizing difference. "The fundamental perversion of politics" stemmed from the fact "it abolishes the basic quality of plurality."[6] For her, politics is not something that emerges in a person or an institution and is then dispersed to other persons. Politics is the very dynamic that unfolds between persons, and that intra-individual aspect is key to her thinking. What she observed in ancient Athens was not politics done by a professional caste from above, but a space in which citizens came together to talk, to listen, and to act.

Ancient Athens showed something that philosophy had forgotten ever since: "Since for the Greeks, the public political space is common to all (*koinon*), the space where the citizens assemble, it is the realm in which all things can first be recognized in their many-sidedness." The very practice of classical Greek democracy truly did justice to the notion of plurality: "The crucial factor is . . . that one gained the ability to truly *see* topics from various sides—that is politically—with the result that people understood how to assume the many possible perspectives provided by the real world."[7]

This spectacular insight has some dramatic consequences. If politics is all about citizens considering issues from various sides in order to shape their futures, then politics is no longer some sort of a necessary evil that allows us to be free, but the very experience of being free! The central tenet of her *Introduction into Politics* therefore is: "The meaning of politics is freedom."[8] She even wrote: "Politics and freedom are identical."[9]

A Pioneer of Democratic Innovation

The consequences for democratic innovation today are far-reaching. Do not separate the many from the few. Do not relegate power to professionals only, as this may risk the origin or thoughtless followers. Do not be satisfied with citizens just controlling government—go for citizens actually shaping government. Do not be satisfied with citizens looking up to their politicians to admire or to despise—have your citizens looking at each other. Do not have citizens tolerating politics as a necessary evil. Lead them into politics, that is, into freedom.

It has often been said that the theoretical groundwork for deliberative democracy, citizens assemblies and sortition-based democracy was formulated by Jurgen Habermas in the 1960s and John Rawls in the 1970s. But the real pioneering work was already done in the 1950s by the woman who lies buried here 100 yards away. She was the true pioneer. In that respect, I concur with Shmuel Lederman, who is going to talk this afternoon, in his analysis on Hannah Arendt and the origins of participatory democracy.[10]

Does that mean that everything is solved now? Arendt called for citizens actively shaping the future of their communities in dialogue with each other, in a way comparable to how it was done in ancient Athens. And now, 70 years later, this is happening in Amsterdam, in Brussels and Paris and Berlin, perhaps soon, even in some of the towns of the Hudson Valley?

Yes, there is reason for some hope about the possible revitalization of democracy through sortition. I've been advocating for deliberative democracy for more than 10 years now, and things have finally started to change and even to accelerate. The OECD published a report last year, bringing together an analysis of citizens assemblies having taken place over the past 20 years, and it documented more than 300. Over the past year and a half since that report was published, another 100 have been added to the list.[11] So, yes, we are witnessing an acceleration.

I was personally involved with designing the permanent Paris Citizens' Assembly that is now being voted on. It has been a fascinating experience, and I remember this summer working in Paris to see a younger generation of Parisian politicians asking experts to go even further in designing a model than they thought possible. But that does not mean that the battle is won.

Internal and External Threats to Revitalization

I see two major threats, an internal one and an external one. Today's electoral democracies are in the process of weakening themselves, perhaps even of killing themselves. The lofty ideals of representative government, and Roger has been so kind to remind them, have turned into the nightmare of party politics with its ongoing and increasing carnival of ritual infighting, highly mediatized performances of difference, an exuberant sense of indignation, and a deeply problematic financing model. A system that was moved to put power in the hands of the most virtuous or the most competent is today often better at getting the worst out of elected representatives than the best.

On top of that: social media, filter bubbles, fake news, echo chambers have polarized entire nations. They have turned the electoral fever into a permanent feature of democracy. They have deeply divided our communities. They have promoted conspiracy thinking. They have eroded trust not only in government, but in each other.

And all this is happening within the framework of neoliberal economies that have widened the gap between the rich and the poor, that have disenfranchised entire social strata, and that have created a largely shared sense of "whatever you vote, it doesn't matter because the system isn't fair." When economies weaken the weak and politics humiliate the humble, it comes as no surprise to see people flock towards those that make them feel proud again and give them a sense of purpose, belonging, and joy.

These are powerful forces and it is far from being sure whether some successful citizens' assemblies taking place in some cities or countries will be enough to make a difference, even if they are successful in bringing reason, respect, curiosity and genuine dialogue back into our democracies.

Populist voters should not be confronted with populist leaders. They are not fascist yet, but they may become so, if we continue to treat them as such. Perhaps populist anger could be redefined as a gift, but a gift wrapped in barbed wire. It's a gift that expresses a willingness of political participation. We can run away from the barbed wire, but we may also try to unwrap and disentangle it.

We should wonder: would a working-class man without a job or college degree, yet who had been given the chance to regularly speak his mind at a citizens' assembly, a place where he feels respected and understood and included as a citizen, would such a man still want to storm the Capital?

During my stay at Bard College, I came across a book containing the final thoughts of Walt Whitman, compiled by a friend during the last years of his life. This is what he had to say about American democracy: "We can't get on with the world of masters: we want men,—a world of men: backbone men—the workers, the doers, the humbles. We want them. . . . They, their like, the crowd of the grave workingmen of our world—they are the hope, the sole hope, the sufficient hope, of our democracy. Before we despair, we have to count them in—after we count them in, we won't despair."[12]

And then a second threat looming over democracy today comes from the outside. Hannah Arendt wondered whether politics as freedom was possible at a moment when the atomic bomb could destroy human civilization at large. Today, we have to ask ourselves whether a deliberative democracy where citizens come together to shape their future is still possible in times of climate crisis. Our predicament is perhaps even more challenging. The clock is ticking and we know what time it is. During the Cold War, one had to reckon with an abstract eventuality of a violent flash. But in times of global warming, we have to live with the concrete reality of a slow, time-delayed destruction.

Is it too late to revitalize democracy, given that the next eight years will be crucial for curbing our greenhouse gas emissions? Is it too late to come together and talk? Part of me is extremely worried about our inertia. Yet, part of me remembers what the IPCC, the United Nations climate panel, said last summer: humans will decide how warm it gets.

Part of me remembers that most people want to live and that a growing number of people are concerned about the future of the planet. Part of me remembers that last year, President Macron organized the Citizens' Convention for the Climate. One hundred and fifty people drafted by a lot came together for months to produce 149 recommendations. It was the boldest, most ambitious and most coherent action plan for climate governance that France had ever seen, a scheme widely endorsed by the public at large. Yet, part of me also remembers that only 15 of the 149 recommendations were enacted upon as such, and that more than half of them were rejected by the French government.

Part of me remembers that last week, the world's very first Global Assembly was launched, a highly promising bottom-up initiative bringing 100 citizens of the world, sampled by lot, to talk about climate change. Part of me hopes that that Global Assembly might become a permanent feature of the United

Nations, so that every year in September, as the General Assembly is taking place, there would also be a Global Assembly. Yet, part of me fears that changing the UN might take much more time than we still have.

Yesterday, I went to visit the place where Hannah Arendt lies buried here on campus. The afternoon light was filtered by the golden foliage. Fallen leaves were cracking under my feet and squirrels were running over the graves as if they had the eternal life. "The meaning of politics is freedom," I remembered. I almost wanted to mumble "thank you." Knowing that she abhorred any form of sentimentality, I would nonetheless have wanted to add "and happy birthday to you, Frau Arendt."

Notes

1. Hannah Arendt, 2005, *The Promise of Politics* (Schocken Books, New York).
2. Mogens Herman Hansen, 1991, *The Athenian Democracy in the Age of Demosthenes: Structures, Principles, and Ideology* (Blackwell, Oxford-Cambridge, Massachusetts).
3. Arendt, *Promise*, pp. 134-5.
4. Ibid., 197.
5. Ibid., 135.
6. Ibid., 94.
7. Ibid., 167.
8. Ibid., 108.
9. Ibid., 129.
10. Shmuel Lederman, 2019, *Hannah Arendt and Participatory Democracy: A People's Utopia* (Palgrave).
11. OECD 2020, Innovative Citizen Participation and New Democratic Institutions: Catching the Deliberative Wave.
12. Brenda Wineapple, 2019, *Walt Whitman Speaks* (Library of America, 105-7).

Arendt and Council Democracy

Shmuel Lederman

Representative Democracy and Colonial Inspirations

Throughout the tradition of political thought until the end of the 18th century, it was well understood that a form of government based on elections would be elitist or "aristocratic" in nature, since the public would tend to vote for those who are more recognizable and "famous," and these would tend to be the rich.[1] Despite the gradual introduction of universal suffrage during the 19th and 20th centuries, this inherent tendency of representative government has not significantly changed, and as many political scientists have recognized, it remains a government by elites. Nevertheless, representative government enjoys wide legitimacy not only as a democratic form of government, but as the only form of democracy possible in the modern world. As Bernard Manin notes: "We are thus left with a paradox that, without having in any obvious way evolved, the relationship between representatives and those they represent is today perceived as democratic, whereas it was originally seen as undemocratic."[2]

To get a better sense of this reconceptualization of the meaning of democracy during the 19th century, it is worthwhile to take a brief look at the democratic thought of the great liberal thinker of that century, John S. Mill.[3] Mill supported democracy, but he struggled to get across to his readers that this is not the kind of democracy we find for example in classic, democratic Athens. The fundamental assumption of supporters of democracy like him, Mill explained on multiple occasions, is that the majority of the public will vote not for people like them, but for people who are better than them, or as Mill puts it in 1831, "the *most highly civilized* portion of the people."[4]

In his 1835 essay, "Rationale of Representation," Mill explains that in order to achieve a responsible government, it is not necessary that the "Many" should themselves be perfectly wise, but only that they be "duly sensible of the value of superior wisdom" and elect those with superior judgment to govern them. Once this is achieved, states Mill, "the argument for universal suffrage . . . is irresistible: for, the experience of ages . . . bears out the assertion, that whenever the multitude are really alive to the necessity of superior intellect, they rarely fail to distinguish those who possess it."[5] As Mill goes on to explain:

> In every country where there are rich and poor, the administration of public affairs would, even under the most democratic constitution, be mainly in the hands of the rich; as has been the

> case in all the republics of the old world, ancient and modern. Not only have the wealthy and leisured classes ten times the means of acquiring personal influence, ten times the means of acquiring intellectual cultivation, which any other person can bring into competition with them; but the very jealousies, supposed to be characteristic of democracy, conspire to the same result. Men are more jealous being commanded by their equals in fortune and condition, than by their superiors.[6]

What we find in Mill, then, is a reconceptualization of the very meaning of democracy as it had been traditionally conceived. The tendency of representative government to bring to power a wealthy elite does not make it undemocratic; on the contrary—this is, as Mill will present it in other writings, the meaning of *rational* democracy, as opposed to false conceptions of democracy some still hold. What distinguishes it from aristocracy is not so much who rules, but the fact that they are accountable to the public through regular elections and thus serve the public interest rather than their own.

In his 1835 review of the first volume of Tocqueville's *Democracy in America*, Mill distinguishes between rational and false democracy in terms of delegation versus representation. The false understanding of democracy is that it is a form of government in which the people elected function as delegates of the people, in the sense that they are supposed to implement the policies decided upon or preferred by those who elect them. The rational understanding of democracy, in contrast, is that it is a form of government in which the elected function as representatives of the people, in the sense that they act for their benefit, are accountable to them and can be dismissed by them after their term ends, but they decide on policies according to their own judgment and the most advanced knowledge of the time, which naturally only a few would possess. This is, for Mill, the crucial difference on which the very institution of democracy hinges. "The substitution of delegation for representation," he writes, "is therefore the one and only danger of democracy."[7] Later in his review, Mill reiterates this point in even stronger terms:

> If democracy should disappoint any of the expectations of its more enlightened partisans, it will be from the substitution of delegation for representation; of the crude and necessarily superficial judgment of the people themselves, for the judgment of those whom the people, having confidence in their honesty, have selected as the wisest guardians whose services they could command. All the chances unfavourable to democracy lie here; and whether the danger be much or little, all who see it ought to unite their efforts to reduce it to the *minimum*.[8]

Mill supported a gradual increase in the working class's representation in government, since he believed that they would gradually come to understand the rational meaning of democracy. He was also genuinely concerned with the just grievances of the workers and knew that unless they were represented, their concerns would not be properly addressed. Furthermore, Mill saw participation in government by representation, as well as by active participation in local government, as having important educational effects.

Indeed, the education of the workers was of the utmost importance to Mill, and he supported a much more extensive popular education.[9] The end of such education, as Mill puts it, is "converting these neglected creatures into rational beings—beings capable of foresight, accessible to reasons and motives addressed to their understanding; and therefore not governed by the utterly senseless modes of feeling and action, which so much astonish educated and observing persons when brought into contact with them."[10] Since many of the British working classes were not yet "rational beings," they posed a problem: "As soon as any idea of equality enters the mind of an uneducated English working man, his head is turned by it. When he ceases to be servile, he becomes insolent."[11]

By the 1850s, Mill's fears of mass democracy were at their peak.[12] In the 1859 essay "Recent Writers on Reform," he clarifies that "those who look the most hopefully to universal suffrage, seldom propose to introduce it otherwise than gradually and tentatively, with the power of stopping short wherever a tendency begins to manifest itself toward making legislation subservient to the misunderstood class interests of labourers and artisans."[13] Not only will this process be gradual, but certain mechanisms that would limit the voting power of the masses must be put in place, first of all an educational threshold for the vote. "If there ever was a political principle at once liberal and conservative," he writes in another essay from 1859, "it is that of an educational qualification."[14] This is because:

> None are so illiberal none so bigoted in their hostility to improvement, none so superstitiously attached to the stupidest and worst of old forms and usages, as the uneducated. None are so unscrupulous, none so eager to clutch at whatever they have not and others have, as the uneducated in possession of power. An uneducated mind is almost incapable of clearly conceiving the rights of others.[15]

Indeed, he concludes, "no lover of improvement can desire that the *predominant* power should be turned over to persons in the mental and moral condition of the English working classes."[16]

Much of Mill's *Considerations on Representative Government* is dedicated to such mechanisms to limit the actual power of the masses in decision making:

denying illiterate persons and those who relied on charity the right to vote; plural voting, which would give the more educated more votes[17]; and proportional representation.[18] As Mill famously put it: "though every one ought to have a voice – that every one should have an equal voice is a totally different proposition."[19]

Mill also insisted that only a few could be charged with the powers to do the actual work of national governance. A network of professional civil servants based on experience, knowledge and expertise would propose and implement legislation and policies, while the function of the elected representatives would be to deliberate and, with regard to legislation but not to administration, to decide on them, as well as to represent the various opinions and interests of the groups within society.[20] Fortunately, Mill had a model to draw on. The East India Company, where he served most of his adult years, proved to be successful in providing India with a government based on knowledge and expertise, while allowing the opinions and interests of the population it governed to be increasingly represented. Indeed, some of Mill's proposals, such as a Council of Legislation or the need for professional civil servants to propose and implement policies, can be traced directly to the institutions of the East India Company.[21]

But as we have seen, these mechanisms served for Mill as *additional* mechanisms to the inherent tendency of representative government to bring about the rule of an elite, strengthened by education that would teach the working classes the right, rational idea of democracy. As Mill reiterates:

> In that falsely called democracy which is really the exclusive rule of the operative classes... the only escape from class legislation in its narrowest, and political ignorance in its most dangerous, form, would lie in such disposition as the uneducated might have to choose educated representatives, and to defer to their opinions. Some willingness to do this might reasonably be expected, and everything would depend upon cultivating it to the highest point.[22]

The "false" idea of democracy, against which Mill wrote so passionately, was not merely a theoretical one: one of the fundamental demands of the Chartist movement, the most important workers' movement in Britain in the mid-19th century, was an annual parliament, to make sure that representatives act as delegates of those who elected them.[23] Moreover, as E. P. Thompson suggested, the mass agitation of the working classes in the 1830s could have resulted in a revolution that might well "have prefigured, in its rapid radicalization, the revolutions of 1848 and the Paris Commune."[24] Increasingly, workers were interpreting Robert Owen in their own terms, turning his proposed "Villages of Co-operation" into self-governing workers' associations.[25] Their aim appears to have been a "form of Syndicalist Government founded on a pyramid system of representation from local lodge to district, and so on to the Trades Parliament."[26] A letter Mill wrote during this period to Brougham about a speech by the Birmingham socialist Attwood might give us a sense of how he saw the possible realization of such radical ideas of the working classes:

> The nonsense to which your lordship alludes about the rights of the labourer to the whole produce of the country, wages, profits, and rent, all included, is the mad nonsense of our friend Hogkins ... These opinions, if they were to spread, would be the subversion of civilized society; worse than the overwhelming deluge of Huns and Tartars.[27]

Note how Mill depicts the threat posed by the possible rise to power of the working classes as a threat to civilization itself. This is, as we have already begun to see, a recurring trope in his writings on the issue. Perhaps the most important example is his call for a reorganization of the reform party in England, in 1839, where he insists that universal suffrage should be dropped as a demand of a newly organized reform party. "One great experiment in government," Mill writes, "is as much as a nation can safely make at a time"; and besides, the middle class cannot be expected to let themselves be "induced to swamp themselves, and hand over to unskilled manual labour the entire powers of the government."[28] Mill praises the more intelligent, enlightened, and moderate parts of the working classes as being the partners of the middle class rather than their enemies. As he puts it:

> [A]re the great and intelligent portion of the Operative classes of whom the London Working Men's Association is representative, are even they themselves free from apprehension of the mass of brutish ignorance which is behind them? of the barbarians whom Universal Suffrage would let in…? Do they never think of the state of the agricultural labourers? of the depraved habits of a large proportion of the well-paid artisans?... Can they wonder that the middle classes ... should tremble at the idea of entrusting political power to such hands? Cannot the intelligent working classes be persuaded, that even for themselves it is better that Universal Suffrage should come gradually? that it should be approached by steps bearing some relation to the progressive extension of intelligence and morality, from the higher to the lower regions of their own manifold domain?[29]

This depiction of a significant portion of the working class as domestic barbarians is extremely significant. Mill was essentially borrowing the colonial discourse, with its distinctions between the civilized and the uncivilized as well as the accepted notion that the uncivilized cannot rule themselves but should be guided by the civilized—to warn against the implications of an unchecked rise of the working classes to governmental power and to reconceptualize representative government based on election as the only rational form of democracy, precisely because it tends to bring to power a civilized elite rather than the domestic barbarians. Mill's democratic theory thus raises the question whether modern democratic theory and practice is at all separable from the European colonial experience and its inspirations, in terms of the mindsets, political norms and forms of governmentality; and to what extent challenging the contemporary model of representative democracy is nothing but a call for the decolonization of democracy.

Arendt and the Councils

As we have seen, from early on in the development of representative democracy there was an alternative conception of the meaning and practice of democracy, which arose from the working classes. Indeed, the vision of a radical participatory democracy in the form of workers councils that emerged in Britain in the 1830s was likely the first appearance of what came to be known as the vision of council democracy. In an important sense, one may argue it was nothing but the translation of the classic meaning of democracy, as it first appeared in democratic Athens, to modern societies—one which contrasted sharply with the "republican" version invented by the Founding Fathers in the United States as well as with the "rational" form of democracy as conceptualized by Mill and others. While during the 1830s in Britain it existed only in the imagination of some radical sections of the working classes, during the 1871 Paris Commune and later on during the European revolutions of the early 20th century, it became an actual reality, even if only for short periods of time. In the second half of the 20th century it was invoked by only a few thinkers outside the socialist tradition, perhaps the most important one was Hannah Arendt.

Arendt's first explicit mention of the councils occurred in the late 1940s, as she was reflecting on the Jewish-Arab war in Palestine. Arendt believed that only a federation based on Jewish-Arab community councils can bring about peace and coexistence between the two peoples.[30] But already in the earlier, 1945 essay titled "Approaches to the 'German Problem'," Arendt cites approvingly the federative ideas of the European resistance movements, and particularly the French resistance's insistence that a federated Europe must be based on "*similarly federated structures in the constituent states*,"[31] namely on the decentralization of the states themselves into smaller public spheres. Already at this early point, then, the councils appear as a "natural" corollary of the broader federal structures Arendt advocated as an alternative to the nation-state, whether in Palestine or in Europe.

It is against this background, as I argue elsewhere,[32] that we need to understand Arendt's oft-cited statement in *The Origins of Totalitarianism*, that "human dignity needs a new guarantee which can be found only in a new political principle, in a new law on earth, whose validity this time must comprehend the whole of humanity while its power must remain strictly limited, rooted in and controlled by newly defined territorial entities."[33] Arendt has in mind here not only a more robust international law and possibly an international court,[34] or the need for the establishment of human plurality as a guiding principle,[35] but also a world based of federations of political communities that are themselves internally decentralized into multiple democratic spaces, in other words: a federations of council democracies.

It is indeed no coincidence that Arendt decided to add her 1958 essay on the Hungarian revolution, in which she celebrates the councils that emerged everywhere during the revolution, as an epilogue to the second edition of *Origins*. Conscious that it might seem odd to readers of *Origins*, she explained:

> The government of total domination certainly corresponds better to the inherent tendencies of a mass society than anything we previously knew. But the council-system clearly has been for a long time the result of the wishes of the people, and not of the masses, and it is just barely possible that it contains the very remedies against mass society and the formation of mass-men for which we look everywhere else in vain.[36]

Arendt makes a similar point in *The Human Condition*:

> What is so easily overlooked by the modern historian who faces the rise of totalitarian systems . . . is that just as the modern masses and their leaders succeeded, at least temporarily, in bringing forth in totalitarianism an authentic, albeit all-destructive, new form of government, thus the people's revolutions, for more than a hundred years now, have come forth, albeit never successfully, with another new form of government: the system of people's councils to take the place of the Continental party system, which, one is tempted to say, was discredited even before it came into existence.[37]

We see, then, that totalitarianism and the council system stood in Arendt's mind as fundamentally opposed forms of governments: the worst and best versions of the two choices—empires or federations—which Arendt believed we had once the nation-state disappeared (as she wrongly anticipated).

As I argue in my book, *Hannah Arendt and Participatory Democracy: A People's Utopia*, the centrality of the vision of council democracy in Arendt's political thought is still underappreciated. While there has been an increasing interest in the council tradition and specifically in Arendt's advocacy of the councils in the last decade, the way her support for this kind of radical, participatory democracy is closely linked to other major themes in her political philosophy remains largely overlooked. Here I can only illustrate this argument. A good place to begin is an exchange between Arendt and Karl Jaspers in 1963. Reflecting on Arendt's book *On Revolution*, Jaspers writes to Arendt:

> Your comparison and identification of the meaning of the 'workers' and 'soldiers' councils, the 'small republics', the beginnings and the truth of all revolutions since the American one, were familiar to me from your Hungary essay. That essay left me hesitant; but now I am convinced of the parallels of meaning and of the opportunity you see in them, though that opportunity has so far always been lost....[38]

The "Hungary" essay is Arendt's 1958 reflections on the Hungarian Revolution, where she celebrates the reappearance of the councils.[39] Later in the letter, Jaspers adds: "I sometimes think in reading your book that Greece is there for you: without your homeland among the Greeks you would hardly have been able to find the form, without them you could not have found the perspective that allowed you to perceive the marvelous significance of the American Constitution and its origins."[40] Jaspers, in other words, reads Arendt's support for a council democracy as motivated by the same inspiration she draws from the Greek polis and its conception of "the political" in *The Human Condition*.

The revealing point is that in her response, Arendt fully approves this reading: "[E]very word you wrote strikes at the very heart of what I meant to say. A tragedy that warms and lightens the heart because such great and simple things were at stake. Heinrich's experience, of course, and the experience of America."[41] "Heinrich's experience" here refers to Arendt's husband Heinrich Blücher's participation in the workers and soldiers' councils in Germany at the end of WWI, as a member of the Spartacus League.[42] Arendt's approval of Jaspers' reading tells us something extremely important: that for Arendt, the potential she saw in the councils was directly related to the meaning of "the political" she attempted to glean from the experience of the Greek polis, in other words: to the very core of her political theory.[43]

Once looked from this perspective, I would argue, several important aspects of Arendt's political theory are seen in a new light. If we recognize that when Arendt analyzes the "space of appearance" in *The Human Condition*, she "primarily has in mind a model of face-to-face human interactions,"[44] then the close connection between the councils and Arendt's understanding of "the political" becomes clearer: what public space could serve as a space where each citizen can reveal who she really is through speech and action in modern democracies, if not an institution like the councils?

Or take, as another important example, Arendt's insistence, especially after the Eichmann trial, that it is thought and judgment—rather than adherence to a preconceived system of values—that might prevent us from participating in evil deeds. This immediately begs the question: what form of government can promote thought and judgment among its citizens? The quite obvious answer is that it is a form of government in which citizens *practice* their judgments and are required to examine and rethink their positions on a regular basis through a constant exchange of opinions with their fellow citizens. A council democracy is precisely the kind of political community that allows and encourages this exchange.

Conclusion

Indeed, I think it can be shown that participatory democracy in the form of a council democracy was in Arendt's mind—sometimes in the background and sometimes in the foreground—as the political form that could realize the potential she saw in the experience of "the political;" as well as when she struggled with the possible political response to some of the tendencies she identified as the roots of some of the most important manifestations of modern evil. Moreover, once Arendt's political theory is seen from this perspective, it emerges as a powerful contribution to the theory of participatory democracy.

Arguably, Arendt is unique in the history of political thought in the kind of qualities she attributes to speech and action in the public sphere—in other words, to "the political"—as a human experience unlike any other. While there is much to criticize in the way she excluded socio-economic questions from the proper content of political discussion and action, this very exclusion also allowed her to go beyond what is commonly understood as the ends of politics and to challenge the very assumptions of modern democratic theory and practice, including among theorists and activists of participatory democracy. While neither Arendt nor participatory democrats ever use/d such terms, once we begin to see the connections between European colonialism and modern democracy, we may come to see Arendt as offering an important path in the effort to decolonize modern democratic theory and practice.

Notes

1. Bernard Manin, *The Principles of Representative Democracy* (Cambridge: Cambridge University Press.1997), p. 133.
2. Ibid., p. 236.
3. In the following discussing I draw on my article, "Representative Democracy and Colonial Inspirations: The Case of John S. Mill," *American Political Science Review*, 2021, doi.org/10.1017/S0003055421001283 (first view)
4. *John S. Mill, Collected Works XXII: Newspaper Writings*, vol. 1, ed. Ann P. Robson and John M. Robson (Routledge & Kegan Paul: University of Toronto Press, 1986), p. 291, emphasis mine.
5. *John S. Mill, Collected Works XVIII: Essays on Politics and Society*, vol. 2, ed. John M. Robson. (Toronto and Buffalo: University of Toronto Press, 1977), p. 24.
6. Ibid., p. 26.
7. Ibid., p. 74
8. Ibid., pp. 79–80, emphasis in the original.
9. *John S. Mill, Collected Works II: Principles of Political Economy with Some of Their Applications to Social Philosophy*, vol. 1, ed. John M. Robson (Routledge & Kegan Paul: University of Toronto Press, 1965), p. 108; pp. 183–84.
10. *John S. Mill, Collected Works IV: Essays on Economics and Society*, vol. 1, ed. John M Robson. (Toronto: University of Toronto Press, 1967), p. 378.
11. Mill, *CW II*, p. 109.
12. Richard Reeves, *John Stuart Mill: Victorian Firebrand* (London: Atlantic Books, 2007), p. 239.
13. John S. Mill, *Collected Works XIX: Essays on Politics and Society*, vol. 1, ed. John M Robson. (Toronto and Buffalo: University of Toronto Press, 1967), p. 350.
14. Ibid., p. 327.
15. Ibid.
16. Ibid.
17. Ibid., pp. 470-79.
18. Ibid., pp. 448-66.
19. Ibid., p. 473.
20. Ibid., pp. 422-34.
21. Ibid., pp. 522-23.
22. Ibid., p. 512.
23. James Epstein and Dorothy Thompson, "Introduction," in *The Chartist Experience: Studies in Working-Class Radicalism and Culture, 1830-60*, eds. James Epstein and Dorothy Thompson (London and Basingstoke: Palgrave Macmillan,1982), p. 8.
24. E. P. Thompson, *The Making of the English Working Class* (London: Victor Gollancz LTD, 1965), p. 817.
25. G. D. H. Cole and Raymond Postgate, *The Common People, 1746-1946* (London: Methuen, University Paperbacks, 1966), p. 242.
26. Pauline Gregg, *Social and Economic History of England, 1760-1965* (London: George G. Harrap & Co. LTD, 1972), pp. 173-74.
27. Quoted in Michael S. J. Packe, *The Life of John Stuart Mill* (London: Secker and Warburg, 1954), p. 101.
28. *John S. Mill, Collected Works VI: Essays on England, Ireland, and the Empire*, ed. John M. Robson (Routledge & Kegan Paul: University of Toronto Press, 1982), p. 482
29. Ibid., p. 488.
30. Hannah Arendt, "To Save the Jewish Homeland," in *Hannah Arendt, The Jewish Writings*, ed. Jerome Kohn and Ron H. Feldman (New York: Schocken Books, 2007), p. 400.
31. Hannah Arendt, "Approaches to the 'German Problem'," in *Essays in Understanding, 1930-1954: Formation, Exile, and Totalitarianism*, ed. Jerome Kohn (New York: Schocken Books, 1994), p. 114, emphasis mine.
32. Shmuel Lederman, *Hannah Arendt and Participatory Democracy: A People's Utopia* (New York: Palgrave Macmillan, 2019), chap. 2.
33. Hannah Arendt, *The Origins of Totalitarianism*, 3rd edition (New York: Harcourt Brace Jovanovich, 1973), ix.
34. See, for example, Roy T. Tsao, "Arendt and the Modern State: Variations on Hegel in The Origins of Totalitarianism," *The Review of Politics 66*, no. 1 (2004): pp. 61-93; Anna Jurkevics,

"Hannah Arendt Reads Carl Schmitt's The Nomos of the Earth: A Dialogue on Law and Geopolitics from the Margins," *European Journal of Political Theory 16*, no. 3 (2017): pp. 345-366.

35. See, for example, *Anya Topolski, Arendt, Levinas and a Politics of Relationality* (London and New York: Rowman and Littlefield International, 2015), p. 68.
36. Hannah Arendt, "Totalitarianism," in *Thinking without a Banister*, ed. Jerome Kohn (New York: Schocken Books, 2018), p. 159.
37. Hannah Arendt, *The Human Condition* (Chicago and London: The University of Chicago Press, 1998), p. 216.
38. Karl Jaspers to Hannah Arendt, May 16, 1963, in *Hannah Arendt, Karl Jaspers: Correspondence, 1926-1969*, ed. Lotte Kohler and Hans Saner, trans. Robert and Rita Kimber (New York: Harcourt Brace & Company, 1992), pp. 504-505.
39. Hannah Arendt, "Totalitarian Imperialism: Reflections on the Hungarian Revolution," *The Journal of Politics 20* (1958): pp. 5-43.
40. *Jaspers to Arendt, in Hannah Arendt, Karl Jaspers*, p. 505.
41. Hannah Arendt to Karl Jaspers, May 29, 1963, in *Hannah Arendt, Karl Jaspers*, p. 507.
42. Elizabeth Young-Bruehl, *Hannah Arendt: For Love of the World*, second edition (New Haven and London: Yale University Press, 2004), p. 125.
43. On the importance of this rarely noted exchange for understanding the origins of Arendt's support for the councils as well as their role in her political thought see also Shmuel Lederman, "Hannah Arendt, The Council Tradition, and Contemporary Political Theory," in Council Democracy: Towards a Democratic Socialist Politics, ed. James Muldoon (New York and London: Routledge, 2018); Shmuel Lederman, "The Centrality of the Councils in Arendt's Political Thought," in *Arendt on Freedom, Liberation and Revolution*, ed. Kei Hiruta (New York: Palgrave Macmillan, 2019).
44. Seyla Benhabib, *The Reluctant Modernism of Hannah Arendt* (London and New Delhi: Sage Publications, 1996), p. 201.

Future Publics: Deliberative Democracies

Michael K. MacKenzie

Today, I'm going to talk about using sortition to represent the future. Many of us are more focused on our near-term concerns than our longer-term interests. We know this as individuals. For example, we eat poorly or exercise too little, even though we know that this is going to negatively affect us in the future. We find it difficult to save for retirement or for emergencies. These are common problems that we have as individuals.

It's even more difficult to act in future-regarding ways as societies. We've done badly, as all of us know, managing long-term issues such as climate change, public debt, nuclear waste disposal, plastics pollution, and natural disaster preparedness. There are many other long-term issues that we're struggling with and have struggled to manage. Many people feel like democracy might be part of the problem rather than part of the solution. And the problem is that democracy has many features that render it shortsighted, or at least this is the concern. There's a sense in which democracy is structurally myopic. It's foundationally myopic and many people have made this argument. But they're actually making a number of arguments at the same time. I've called this the democratic myopia thesis, and I've identified at least four arguments within this thesis. And often these arguments are presented at the same time. They're presented as one set of arguments, but actually they're different types of arguments. They're conceptually distinct.

The first one has to do with myopic voters. If we are myopic, if we care more about the near-term than the long-term, then politicians, elected officials who are acting in the interests of the people who are trying to do what the people demand, are going to be shortsighted as well.

Now, this argument is often conflated with the next one, which is the short electoral cycles argument. But actually, these are two conceptually distinct arguments. In this case, politicians have a strong incentive not to invest in the future precisely because they know in a democratic system that future governments will have opportunities to undermine the long-term investments they're making to undermine long-term plans or to reverse their decisions in the future. There's a strong incentive not to invest in the future, even if you know that it should be done.

A third argument is an ontological one, future generations are not included or rather cannot be included in our decision-making processes today. This is a problem, of course, for all political systems, but it's a conceptual problem and a problem of principle for democracies because democracies are supposed to include affected publics. That is, they're supposed to adhere to the all-affected principle, which says that all those who are affected by collective decisions should have some meaningful role in making those decisions. Now, we can't even live up to that. We can't even approximate that principle when it comes to including future generations simply because they don't exist. But if they don't exist, then their interests and concerns are likely to be ignored or at least undervalued in the collective decisions that we make.

The fourth argument that's often cited has to do with Democratic capture, and this is the idea that there may be interests or groups within society who have specific short-term objectives that they wish to pursue at the expense of the longer-term interests of society as a whole. Now, there are different versions of this argument, but one has to do with powerful economic actors, both individuals and corporations. And the idea here is that if those actors have distinct short-term interests that they wish to pursue, they will be able to advance those interests at the expense of the longer-term interests of society as a whole. It's true that most democratic systems, and I think Kali was referencing this, most democratic systems have been captured in this way by powerful economic actors. People have seen this as a possible source of the democratic myopia that I'm talking about.

These are the four arguments that make up the democratic myopia thesis. But you might have noticed that they're very different and are predicated on different assumptions. According to the first two arguments, democracies will be shortsighted when they're working well, and this is partly why people are so concerned about this issue: that democracies will be shortsighted precisely when they're doing what they're supposed to be doing. That is to say, when they're responsive to the demands of voters and when elected politicians are accountable and may be replaced by new ones in the future.

According to the second two arguments, democracies will be shortsighted when they're working poorly, which is to say when they fail to be inclusive or inclusive in the right ways and are insufficiently responsive to the demands of affected publics. And so, these are problems, but they're different problems, and they're predicated on different assumptions about how democracy works. But the persuasiveness of the democratic myopia thesis has led many people to think that democracy is part of the problem, not part of the solution. It's part of the problem if we're trying to act in future regarding ways.

Some people have argued that what we need are authoritarian regimes in order to make our political systems more future regarding. Regimes that have the power and capacity to impose near-term costs on unwilling publics for their own future benefit. I'm more interested in democratic solutions to the democratic myopia problem. The question is how can we make our democratic systems more concerned with the future while also making them more democratic? And that's a really difficult question. It's unclear how we can do that.

I do think that sortition may be part of the solution. We've already talked a lot about sorting chambers. But just imagine for the purposes of this argument, a political system with two legislative assemblies. One is an elected assembly and the other is a permanent sortition chamber. I'm delighted to hear that today Paris seems to have voted to create something like this. This sort of system could be applied at the local, regional, national, or even international levels. You can imagine the randomly selected legislature sitting for some limited period of time, maybe one or two years. I think that the people who sit in the chamber should be paid just like the other politicians and empowered. They would, in this scenario, have the power to assess, approve, amend, and reject more proposals coming from the elected assembly.

But this randomly selected assembly should also have the power to initiate its own law proposals, which would then be assessed and deliberated in the elected assembly as well. Now, here's the catch. I think this kind of institution should be given an explicit mandate to act as a representative of the future. We don't have an institution like this in any of our political systems.

This particular model, sortition, a randomly selected permanent sortition legislature, has a number of features that I think are particularly well suited for representing the future. First, it would be inclusive. It would be more representative of all the different types of people in society. And this is important because when we're making long-term decisions, we're not just making decisions about climate and climate action or debt or any of the things that I've mentioned already. Every decision that we make has some long-term consequences, which is why I think we need a general purpose randomly selected legislature with an explicit mandate to represent the future.

But it's even more complicated than that. Every decision that we make as a society will affect different groups within our current publics and also different groups and interests in future publics. The best way to get at how these long-term decisions are going to affect different groups both now and in the future is to have an inclusive representative assembly. Secondly, it would be deliberative. The research shows that these sorts of deliberative assemblies that we've been talking about today are in fact, highly deliberative. And this matters because our biases against the future are located in the intuitive parts of our brains, which is to say that we're biased against the future when we're not thinking carefully enough. The thing about deliberation is that it forces us into cognitively demanding situations. We have to think about what we're arguing for. We have to listen to the arguments of others. We have to formulate our own arguments in ways that people might plausibly accept. These are cognitively demanding tasks, and they force us to start using the analytical parts of our brains. And when we use the analytical parts of our brains, the biases we have against the future are harder to sustain. The expectation is that the people coming into this assembly would be just as myopic as anybody else, but they wouldn't be as myopic once they start talking to each other in this deliberative assembly.

And thirdly, it would be independent in at least two ways. One, it wouldn't be subject to the kinds of political dynamics associated with the short electoral cycles that I just talked about. But secondly, the members of the Citizens Assembly could act independently from, for example, wealthy individuals or interests who seek to capture them and persuade them to vote in particular ways. They would have very little leverage over people who are part of a randomly selected legislature, because the members wouldn't go to wealthy interests for their positions on the legislature. Wealthy interests wouldn't have supported their election campaigns. There's a sense in which these randomly selected representatives could act independently. And in fact, the chance, the idea of selecting people randomly, underscores this kind of independence. The whole purpose or one of the purposes of random selection is to support this autonomy or independence that people have.

And then fourthly, this body would be empowered. As I've explained, I think it could be designed so that it reviews legislation, but also may be empowered to veto it or initiate its own future regarding legislation. We simply don't have a democratic representative, a deliberative institution that is charged with representing the interests of the future, but is also empowered in our existing democratic systems.

I don't think a randomly selected legislature can solve all of our problems, but it would be a significant improvement over what we currently have in most of our legislative systems. There are other really interesting democratic innovations that people are talking about that would help enhance our capacities to act in future regarding ways. Nevertheless, I think that a randomly selected sortation chamber at the local, regional, national, and international levels, can help ensure that the interests of future others are not ignored in our collective decision-making processes.

Q&A with Michael MacKenzie and Shmuel Lederer
Moderator: Yasemin Sari

Yasemin Sari: The first question has to do with the inclusion or the criterion of inclusion in these councils or chambers that perhaps may be expanded beyond our citizenship requirements to include noncitizens, or other people who may have lost their political rights, or are not able to meaningfully exercise them, as we've heard from previous discussions as well. The second question is about justification. In both your instances, justification seems to have very high stakes. I wonder if you'd like to speak to that? How does that justification work in this conversation in the council or chamber?

Michael MacKenzie: I think this idea that these randomly selected bodies have a role to play in helping navigate a kind of politics of diversity is a really good point. This is how I think about politics as well. I mean, politics is what happens when we have to navigate disagreements among people and we have different tools of doing that. Some of them are objectionable on normative grounds like violence. It's still a political tool.

This is something Arendt was trying to argue against. I think that violence is a political tool. There are other normatively better ways of dealing with violence, and these kinds of assemblies do bring people into environments that normalize working through differences in productive ways.

I want to push back a bit on some of the conversation we had earlier with respect to treating these as participatory institutions. They could be in the way that Roger was talking about earlier. If you have a kind of nested structure, where there's assemblies all over the place and people, we'll have many opportunities to participate, and I very much support that kind of approach or at least experiments in that area.

Nevertheless, the assemblies that are being run, and the one that looks like it might be built in Paris, or the kind of assembly I was imagining in my talk, are not particularly participatory institutions. Only a very small number of the public would ever be involved. I think they are representative institutions, they're just representative in different ways.

Something else I've been trying to push back on is this tendency of democratic theorists to use citizens in place of people or individual or groups. I feel particularly sensitive about that because I live in the United States and I'm not a citizen. I have no official role to play in politics here. But that doesn't mean I don't—and this is something that Arendt would emphasize—I don't have opportunities for political action within this political community.

Citizen assemblies, as they were run in Canada, were predicated, I think, for good reason, on the voter list because we have reasonably good voter lists there, and that's a good way of identifying the population and the assemblies in Canada, where on electoral reform, so it made sense. But you could have assemblies that are open to anybody who's part of the community. I think it's a really important way of thinking about how we revitalize democracy, which is what we're talking about here this week—about how we can start getting out of this confinement that we have and this obsession with democracy being for citizens. If we define citizens as a kind of legal group who have the right to vote that's not a big enough group, and it's not an accurate description of most of our societies.

Shmuel Lederer: First of all, I think for a while the councils challenged sovereignty, the idea of sovereignty, and were supposed to promote plurality in several dimensions. The more obvious ones were that the councils are a decentralized institution. There will be less concentration of power within the government or other centralized institutions for that matter. Sovereignty in the sense of the centralization of power was one dimension which the councils were supposed to serve, as is anti-sovereignty institution.

The other quite obvious way was that in the council, citizens, and perhaps also noncitizens, were supposed to exchange opinions. And for Arendt, exchanging opinions, seeing the point of view of the other, perhaps changing your point of view, was the very essence of politics. It was when you emphasized or the reason that she emphasized that because she believed we were not sovereign, right? We were dependent on others to sharpen our opinions to get a richer understanding of the world. So, that's another dimension.

The third and perhaps more interesting dimension for Arendt would be, as Tracy said before in a previous session, there is no "we." The "we" is more complicated than we commonly speak about it. Arendt would say there is no "I," right? What is the "I?" How we experience ourselves is different when we talk to each other in the public sphere. The "I" is not a solid entity. It's something that changes. It's something that appears differently when we are in our private sphere than when we are in the public sphere. That kind of challenging the sovereignty of the self. We are not masters of our own identity in in that sense. In all these dimensions, the councils are kind of challenging the very notion of sovereignty.

Now, with regard to the question of noncitizens, that's a very interesting and complicated one, because there is something that the very notion of citizenship creates a "we" as something a solid in our lives, in the modern world. To bring in noncitizens, we need perhaps a new concept of communal identity or national identity or not national identity. I think Arendt was not there. We should be there. Arendt was not there yet, perhaps because following the Holocaust, she was acutely aware of the benefits of citizenship, so she very much emphasized this kind of a political belonging. We should probably go beyond that.

YS: I love that phrase. Maybe reimagining what it means to belong and creating spaces of belonging differently.

Audience Question: The social categories that we use are complicated and overlapping, and I worry about issues of tokenism. For example, Muslim people in the United States represent only about one percent of the population. If you have a group of 100 and you only have one Muslim representative, then the needs of that group are very much not represented. It's a multifaceted group that has different Muslim people with different opinions on things, of course.

As you know, we were talking earlier about Ireland, with voting on gay rights and gay marriage, you know, necessarily LGBTQ people are a minority. Any sort of representative council or community that is talking about gay marriage rights, and that is trying to represent the broad swath of people, are going to be mostly people who are not of that group making decisions for that group.

I wonder, thinking along the lines of citizenship, if these groups are only citizen-based, then what about questions about undocumented immigrants in the United States? We've seen recently the atrocities that can happen when those people's concerns are not considered by elected officials in the ways in which violence can be perpetrated against those communities. How do we reckon with these sorts of multifaceted ways that identity is created, and with these sorts of questions of representation, tokenism, and citizenship?

MM: I agree with you, and I think it emphasizes something that we talked about earlier after David Ven Reybrouck's talk, which is this tension between stratification and random selection. On one level, random selection is brilliant because it does get at all these complicated, overlapping forms of identity. That is, if you have a large enough group and you use random selection to form that group, you should, at least in principle, get people of all different types, people who have different overlapping identities or conceptions of themselves. And so, on one level, random selection or sortition addresses precisely the concern that you're raising.

But on another level, it doesn't, which is also the point you wanted to make, which is that sometimes there are groups that have real interests that need to be addressed, who wouldn't make up a sufficiently large number within any particular randomly selected assembly. And this then emphasizes this tension, which Roger and David were talking about earlier, about when to use stratification and how much and when to use pure random processes.

I think there's no specific answer to that, but if you're talking about an issue-specific kind of assembly, an issue that has to do, for example, with relations that Muslim Americans have with other Americans, or people more generally, or religious issues in general, these sorts of assemblies might call for stratification processes that make sure enough people from the Muslim community are included. Now, this wouldn't be possible for the kind of general-purpose assembly that I was talking about, but it would be possible for many of these issue specific assemblies. And that is in fact what we've done.

At lunch, we were talking about the fascinating global assembly, and they're using opinions about climate change to select participants because they want to make sure that people who are skeptical about climate change, and options for dealing with it, are sufficiently included so that the conversation can include them and it can be a real conversation about the existing tensions about that issue that exist more broadly in our society. I think it comes back to that tension between stratification, when to do it, and random selection, and when to use pure random processes.

SL: Representation itself, in the sense of who should be represented and how, is itself a political question, right? It can't constantly change according to how we perceive what kind of identities are especially important to us and should be represented. I think, at the very least, something like a more participatory democracy in institutions like councils or citizen assemblies allow a more direct and more open discussion about what kind of identities we think should be represented and are not represented in our democracy. It gives more space, at the very least, to the question of representation.

David Van Reybrouck: A short remark and two short questions. I very much like Michael when you said that the notion of citizens should be expanded or that the categories of people who are eligible should be more than just citizens. In the first institutionalized permanent citizens assembly in the German-speaking part of Belgium, people can be younger than with classical voting rights. You can vote from age 18 onwards; for the citizens assembly, being 16 is enough. And secondly, you don't need to be a Belgian or have a Belgian permit of residence, so anyone living there can actually be drafted by law.

For Shmuel, have you come across anything Hannah Arendt has written on sortition? Was her idea on how Athenian democracy worked, a rather vague impression, without knowing the intricacies of how it worked?

For Michael, you presented this great idea of sortition chambers serving the future. You have done empirical research on this. I read your article. Can you share a little bit about the insights you have from what a random sample can do for the future?

SL: I don't think Arendt was very much interested in the specific mechanisms that were in Athens or in the Greek polis, and this is why she doesn't write about sortition and so on, because she was interested in the why and the justification, in the legitimation question. The important question was why we need, for example, democracy in the specific way that she thought about democracy. I think one of her great innovations was that it was not about getting our interest realized or getting power, and so on. There is a certain human experience that we can experience through politics or through speaking and acting with each other that does not exist in any other sphere. She was interested in the Greek polis or in Athens because she tried to recover this answer that she thought was completely forgotten in the Western tradition. Again, as far as I recall, she didn't write about this specific mechanism, but rather the meaning of the political for the Greeks.

MM: The work that I did with my colleague was a laboratory experiment where we tested that and were focused specifically on climate-action policy. We asked people whether they'd be willing to pay now for future potential benefits. But we didn't have everybody do the same thing. We had 50 groups of between five and eight people in each group, and half of those groups were randomly assigned to deliberate and half didn't deliberate. We found, for example, that the people who deliberated climate-action policies were significantly more willing to pay near-term costs for future potential benefits and in particular on gasoline taxes, so taxes at the pump. People were significantly more willing to pay substantially more at the pump after deliberating.

Our sample of people who participated in the experiment, about 330 in total, were evenly split on that issue coming in. About 50 percent of people thought that it was a good idea to increase gas taxes and 50 percent didn't. Those who deliberated became significantly more willing to support those than those who didn't.

Democracy Reinvented: Participatory Budgeting and Civic Innovation in America

Hollie Russon Gilman

I was reflecting about the origins of my research and how much Hannah Arendt had inspired me. As an undergraduate at the University of Chicago, I was steeped in Arendt's writings and took courses from people like Herman Sinaiko, who actually studied with her. When I began my research on participatory forms of democracy, a lot of Arendt's thinking around the *polis,* and about how humans' unique ability for speech enables the conditions for freedom, played a role in my research. I'm going to outline three opportunities and lessons I see in my research on participatory democracy in the United States.

To begin, I will invoke Arendt's quote that, "to be political, to live in a polis, meant that everything was decided through words and persuasion and not through force and violence." And, for me, a lot of this research is about how we connect people at the local level and how to reimagine smaller scale democracy. For Plato, 5,040 people was the maximum number of people for a unit of government and the *polis*, with both its strengths and weaknesses such as large barriers to entry and marginalization of many communities, was inescapably local.

There is an opportunity now for developing what I refer to in my recent coauthored book *Civic Power* as "hooks and levers" between communities and decision makers to deepen cogovernance models. The local level is a critical aspect. In the past year, the demands for racial justice and the COVID crisis have redoubled the impact and the awareness that locality is more central than ever to our civic and communal lives.

With respect to models of cogovernance, the following questions arise: how do we equip not just civil society, but everyday people in their communities? And how do we build in those hooks and levers into decision making so that there is accountability, pressure, and positive feedback loops between what people are demanding and asking for, but also what the government can deliver? The example of participatory budgeting stands out to me as an opportunity to really tap into people's hyper-local expertise.

Participatory budgeting in the United States has placed the emphasis on capital allocations, brick and mortar places where people in their neighborhoods can come out to be seen and heard. The process of participatory budgeting was imported from Brazil in 1989 after a 20-year military dictatorship and has been gaining momentum in the United States, with one Chicago alderman in 2009 putting a portion of his menu money discretionary dollars back into the hands of residents.

When I worked in the White House at the Office of Science Technology Policy in the Obama administration, I led our open-government innovation agenda exploring how the United States, as a global partner, works to advance open government around the world, but also domestically. Can we think about what that could look like? And are there opportunities with high dollars to inject participatory budgeting? That conversation is more relevant than ever with recovery dollars in infrastructure spending, and I'll talk a little bit about civic infrastructure in a minute, but thinking about where are those opportunities? New York has been the largest implementor of participatory budgeting in North America to date,[1] allocating over $35 million in funding in 2019 alone[2] (the City temporarily suspended participatory budgeting in the first year of the COVID-19 pandemic but has since reinstated the program in various districts[3]).

During COVID, in large part, that process has come to a halt. It will be interesting to see if and how that process can gain momentum as an opportunity for people to be experts in their locality and to take the size of government decision making and put it to a place that is manageable. And to also ensure that the questions decision makers are asking of everyday residents are whether they can be experts in places such as parks and recreation centers. What transportation do you need in your community, for example? Because I fear that too often, we do not engage residents in ways that are productive or that actually tap into their knowledge and that can lead to real outcomes. And that requires resetting expectations and decision makers being much more transparent and upfront with people in their communities.

That brings me to my second lesson, which is the opportunity to think about bureaucratized participation within these government decision-making bodies. We're seeing a push for this on the federal level. A year ago, the Biden-Harris administration passed several high-level and critical executive orders and issued a request for information to enhance and strengthen documents, most notably on racial equity,[4] in order to transform federal customer experience,[5] and modernize regulations and rulemaking.[6] Since then, the Office of Management and Budget has made progress toward bringing consultation and engagement with historically underserved communities into federal agencies to modernize the regulatory process. There is much left to learn from practitioners and academics about best practices for effective and equitable engagement, but this is an important opportunity that is happening across the federal government.

In cities and localities, you're seeing innovation offices being embedded and launched, and I think there are questions about if and how these offices can create opportunities for residents to engage in the decision-making process. Some have more opportunities for engagement than others, moving beyond lip service or PR campaigns, thinking about ways where there's actually skin in the game in terms of what these decisions look like. There are a few offices that come to mind when I think about this. Boston's Office of Mechanics has been an innovator in reaching out to the community. For example, when they've thought about middle-income housing, they actually built little housing units and drove them out to the community to have people walk through them and share their input and expertise.

New York City, through a ballot initiative, launched the first civic engagement commission to institutionalize public engagement. The remit is both community board engagement, but also participatory budgeting. And this is not just happening on the East Coast, you're seeing this all across the country. Places are trying to embed these offices. Detroit has created a position of Chief Storyteller for the City.[7]

There are different offices in the municipal governments where there is an opportunity to widen the aperture of what traditional local government looks like and how it can create that space for hooks and levers to acquaint residents and in particular, traditionally marginalized voices, especially Black and Brown communities, in the decision-making process.

My final point is about the practice of democracy, and places that offer an opportunity for people to come together and strengthen our civic muscles. As part of this work, I'm leading the working group for the American Academy of Arts and Sciences' "Our Common Purpose[8]" report. There was one recommendation to imagine what it would look like to launch a trust for civic infrastructure that could fund people, programs, and places to support practices of democracy. The last year has underscored the power of public spaces, both virtual and in person, for how people engage and understand their democratic life.

For example, the Civic Commons Initiative is a donor collaborative of key sites in Akron, Chicago, Detroit, Memphis, and Philadelphia, bringing together national funders and local partners to reimagine spaces. An initiative that I'm very interested in is RUX, which is in Kentucky and stands for the Rural Urban Exchange. It's a creative leadership program to build confidence, social capital, bridge divides, unite Kentuckians, and have people come together for about 75 hours of programming over the year. It's focused on people, places, and partnerships.

I'm going to wrap up with a quote that I love from RUX participant, Ashley Smith: "I love the intention of RUX going into different communities and seeking out the hidden figures who are really making that community, city, or town thrive. And as always, it's the folks really at the margins operating on less than what they actually need and doing incredible things with that."[9]

There is obviously no one panacea to strengthen our civic muscles and to build more opportunities and mechanisms for collaborative participatory democracy, but I have been inspired that I'm seeing more demand signals on behalf of the decision makers in these seats of power. I think there is a clear demand signal from people that they want to be more fully engaged in these processes.

Q&A Session

Thomas Bartscherer: It's one of the marvels and glories of the Arendt Center and of Roger's work generally that it has such a big tent and there are so many things brought together in this conference. I'm aware of the emphasis on very abstract theoretical concerns and also very particular practical concerns. And also, as Roger said at the beginning of the conference, the focus on a burgeoning discourse around deliberative democracy linked to a tradition of civic republicanism in an Arendt spirit, and I think one of the things we see in this panel is two very different talks that can be intersected and brought into relation with one another in ways that I won't be able to do, but hopefully you will.

I do have a couple of questions, but I feel like one point of intersection between these two talks is the significance of the local. Hollie, your first point was on the importance of the local for these initiatives. And obviously that's central to James's remarks as well. Hollie, you mentioned the role of the chief storyteller. And I think something about storytelling links these two as well. Hollie, my question for you comes in part from what you gave us to read in the reader for the conference—about participatory budgeting and how that would work. You talked about the advantages that it brings and you raised the point that it requires decision makers to be willing to give up some of their power. What is the incentive as you understand it, for decision makers to give? Is it the carrot and stick? Is it the threat of not being elected? How is that achieved? What's the incentive for them or the fear that they're responding to? I welcome you to address one another as you wish.

James, you brought something to the conference that I haven't heard much talk of yet, which is about the past. This conference is very much about the future and about possibility. And your focus is on something that is passed and is lost, and the emphasis on the need to recognize and face the loss. I'm wondering if you can say more about why that needs to be done? Why not simply look forward? We have these problems and we're looking for solutions. It seems like you have an intuition about there being some profound fault in the way we would proceed if we don't begin with a recognition of the loss. I'm not sure I understand at least why that's necessary, why we can't just move forward from where we are. Hollie, I invite you first to respond.

Hollie Russon Gilman: These are great questions, and I also appreciated and learned a lot from your presentation. I think that connection between Arendt and Wendell and then Jefferson was really interesting. And I appreciate what we were saying about Roger's point around the deliberative discourse connected to the world of practice. I have a few quick thoughts on this, and it will tie back to your question.

James, listening to your talk, when I think of what was lost in the past year and a half and people feeling like they weren't able to escape those confined roles to be in the polis, and thinking of Unger's interpretation of Arendt here that the escape from our confined roles is an expression of freedom. Is there an opportunity to look for more expressions of freedom? And so, to your question, what are the incentives for our elected officials? I think there's many.

I think the last year and a half have shifted them as well. When I was working on these questions and engaging with local leaders, too often there is a perception that leaders are going to open Pandora's box, which results in fear of engaging the public without translating that engagement into action. I think part of what that requires for a mitigation strategy is having more transparency mechanisms so that people can be upfront about what's on the table and what is not, about seeing the proverbial sausage being made.

When you look at something like participatory budgeting, it's a hands-on civics education and it's reduced the barriers of who can vote in the United States. The process is opened up to people as young as 12 years old. I've seen people volunteering their time after hours to explain to young people how the Department of Transportation in a given city does its policymaking. Given the crisis of our democracy and the clear lack of trust and legitimacy facing so many government decision-making bodies, there is an incentive for new processes. This requires people with decision-making power wanting to widen the aperture and open it up towards more transparent and legitimating forms of governance.

There is also an effectiveness argument to be made. People in their own local communities have specific knowledge and storytelling abilities and can convey that information in a way that is free from special interests and traditional entrenched power. Policy makers can tap into local knowledge and expertise toward better outcomes. There is also an incentive for decision makers to create more forms of deliberative, participatory democracy to address the real crisis of trust and lack of legitimacy in governance. I'll turn it over to James.

James Barry Jr.: I wanted to say that Hollie and I had a chance to talk last week. I agree with your comments, Thomas, that there is this important overlap in what we're doing and it does bear on the local. I think I'm happy that Hollie and people working in the areas that she's working with are optimistic. I will admit that I'm probably not optimistic when it comes to the local, and I'm tempted to say that as I was hinting in my comments earlier, the local has been impoverished in important ways. Has lost its power in important ways. These are things, of course, that Jefferson was worried about. This is why he thought small government was important, and why he thought the word "republics" were the living heart of representative democracy. We have to work on all fronts on this.

To your question, Thomas, and like Hollie, I think it's an important question. As a matter of fact, it's a question I asked when I gave the first version of this paper at the Arendt Circle two years ago in Edmonton. It was labeled, and I'm sure it was meant in the best possible way, as a kind of defunct nostalgia. I want to get T-shirts made in a nice bright purple anyway. This is a problem. When we look to the past, I think there's a tendency to think of it as nostalgia. My argument is not an original one, it's borrowed from Arendt, and I think we all know it well from *On Revolution*, where she talks about the lost treasure. And this lost treasure is not something that I think she thinks we should say, you know, we should have a funeral for and be done. I think we're obliged.

This is the exhortation, as I read it, that we're obliged to look at it. We need to understand what happened in terms of US agricultural policy in 1952. We need to understand the strange, ambivalent, nature of the Land Act of 1862. We need to understand the way in which the question of land is at the heart of the Civil War. We need to understand all of those things. And if we're not engaging in that conversation, then I don't think there's very much we can do to move forward that's not going to backfire on us. That's the short version. I'm tempted to ask Hollie, for you to respond, but I think I ought to open to the audience.

Audience Member: Thanks very much to all three. I have maybe a red herring of a question, which is really about the status of the urban in your thinking, and particularly, Dr. Barry's. I kept thinking that the nostalgia for a kind of agrarian land possession. I use that word nostalgia with quotes around it, and it worried me because for one thing, it seemed to point to a certain kind of privilege. Those people who get to own land are totally privileged. But the other side of it is what happens in your thinking, to the urban, to the whole idea of a kind of that comes, I guess, was most powerful in the 20th century and now in the 21st century, I think it is a real active question. I address that question to both of you. James, maybe you can begin.

JB: This is a question that's going to require a lot of talk. Especially in the last few years, we've seen this kind of polarization, political polarization, between the urban and the rural, which is based upon stereotypes of a certain sort. But there's no denying that if you look at something as crude as census data from 1800 to 2000, you see the shift. In Jefferson's time, less than 10 percent of the people lived in an urban setting. In our time, it's about 80 percent or something like that. And many of the people who live under the census label of rural are not actually rural. They just live in smaller sorts of suburban or urban tracts.

We've had this dramatic shift going from the rural to the urban as a sort of general orientation. I think the question still stands in terms of urban life, because it's still this notion of place. This is why you have, for example, urban gardens. You have people who recognize the importance of land, parks, and so on, in ways that are really important. That is no way to deny the importance of this question. It needs to be talked about in a broad-based way.

HRG: It's a really great question. I was thinking about some of the work I'm doing on trying to build a national trust for civic infrastructure working with rural and urban communities. I'm thinking about what can unite us, where there are more commonalities, and, especially, where have we learned lessons from the pandemic. I'm thinking of some critical functions that are required as the undergirding of democracy, whether it's broadband access or paid family leave.

Are there places where there's almost too much emphasis placed on the urban rural dichotomy? Granted, there are real questions of equity and our historic racism that need to be addressed, but are there also opportunities for recognizing that there are some commonalities in what is required for revitalizing democracy in both of these places? Thank you.

Moderator: I'm reminded that Roger asked speakers to introduce themselves. The previous question was from Ann Lauterbach and the next is from Thomas Field. Thank you.

Audience Member: My question follows up on this previous discussion about the status or the way you understand the local. I would like to hear more about that, possibly in the following way. James, this is mostly a question for you, but essentially for both of you, since you base your reading or suggestions also on a reading of Arendt, and there's an interesting tie back to the previous panel. Of course, the words are an example of an experience of political action, not necessarily a model, but an example from which experience can be drawn, so to speak, and that one of the characteristics is that the poll list is everywhere, so to speak, where people come together and act, not necessarily where they're routed. My question is very much about your understanding of a rootedness or a possibility of a nomadic, let's say, shape of this community that acts together. And the connected question of that is maybe too obvious and you might ignore it if it's too obvious. I was wondering, James, if for you, the assemblies would be a way that have been discussed earlier all day of a revitalized or a political action that you could see within your framework or you see that rather in attention to that if we think of the discussion earlier, that citizens could also be understood as people who are not actually citizens, live there are rooted but come through and still participate. Thank you.

TB: Since this is directed primarily at James, I'll invite you, James, to respond first, but then, Hollie, you as well.

JB: This is another question that deserves a very, very, very long discussion over and over again by many people. The question, as I've been thinking about it and discussing with people, has to do with the status of different groups of people in this country, whether they be a Native American or African American or whatever. And what's interesting is that there is this shared view, at least on the part of significant numbers. I'm thinking of the land back movement, for example, among certain tribes, there's this importance of the land as a grounding principle. That doesn't mean that we're trapped on a specific locale, but it's the place from which we begin. And it's the place before we're adults that I think we get our bearings. The question of education comes into this as well. I think that the question of rootedness, as Thomas mentioned, is very important here. And as we all know from the beginning of her work, at least with the original preface to the totalitarianism book, she's concerned about these problems of ruthlessness and powerlessness, and she links them all together.

The status of refugees can also be brought into this, and the need for a grounding and land. This is a question that can't be answered by any one person. My effort is only to remind us that at least to this point in history, the way in which communities seem to be defined has this legacy in number one, land-based community, but number two, the loss of land-based communities. This ambivalent legacy that we've been given. I'll leave it at that.

Moderator: And Hollie, I see the looming timekeeper, so I think you're going to have the last word here. You're welcome to respond to the question, also, anything else you might want to say.

HRG: These are such rich questions. I think it's really interesting this idea of the definition to land them in opposition to it. Unfortunately, we won't have enough time to discuss it but I'm thinking of the large-scale online deliberative democracy forums that I've been a part of and done a lot of research on. We are seeing governments use these platforms for more participatory democracy. There may be an opportunity to foster a more transnational identity, while also recognizing the locality of place and the primacy of thought and how to hold that tension. At the same time, we have to understand that opportunity is part of this broader movement and moment to tie around in this deliberate democracy discourse. I think the role of digital public spaces and addressing those inequities within is going to be essential.

Thank you so much.

Notes

1. New York City Council (press release), "Speaker Melissa Mark-Viverito and New York City Council Launch 2015-2016 Participatory Budgeting Cycle," September 21, 2015. Retrieved from: archive.org/web/20151126195511/http://council.nyc.gov/html/pr/092115launch.shtml
2. New York City Council, Participatory Budgeting. Retrieved from: council.nyc.gov/pb/
3. Sandoval, Gabriel, "City Council Members Bringing Back Participatory Budgeting for Some, Not All," *The City*, March 22, 2021. Retrieved from: thecity.nyc/2021/3/22/22343716/nyc-participatory-budgeting-city-council-covid
4. The White House, Executive Order on Advancing Racial Equity and Support for Underserved Communities through the Federal Government, January 20, 2021. Retrieved from: whitehouse.gov/briefing-room/presidential-actions/2021/01/20/executive-order-advancing-racial-equity-and-support-for-underserved-communities-through-the-federal-government/
5. The White House, Executive Order on Transforming Federal Customer Experience and Service Delivery to Rebuild Trust in Government, December 13, 2021. Retrieved from: whitehouse.gov/briefing-room/presidential-actions/2021/12/13/executive-order-on-transforming-federal-customer-experience-and-service-delivery-to-rebuild-trust-in-government/
6. The White House, Modernizing Regulatory Review, January 20, 2021. Retrieved from: whitehouse.gov/briefing-room/presidential-actions/2021/01/20/modernizing-regulatory-review/
7. City of Detroit, "Eric Thomas Joins the City of Detroit as Chief Storyteller," January 28, 2020. Retrieved from: detroitmi.gov/news/eric-thomas-joins-city-detroit-chief-storyteller#:~:text=-DETROIT%20%2D%20Eric%20Thomas%2C%20a%20lifelong,prestigious%20fellowship%20at%20Stanford%20University.
8. amacad.org/ourcommonpurpose/report
9. RUX, Living with Complexity: Five years of the Kentucky Rural-Urban Exchange, August, 2020, p. 65. Retrieved from: static1.squarespace.com/static/57f4009b9de4bbad72bcfb32/t/5f31b094a4de330896ae62b7/1597092023726/RUX+Case+Study+-+Final.pdf

Local Affections and Worldly Love: Hannah Arendt and Wendell Berry on the Resistance of Belonging

James Barry Jr.

> These attitudes issue from the great blank in the political-industrial mind that has forgotten, if it ever knew, the public and political value of securing for all citizens a reasonable permanence of dwelling place and vocation. . . .
> —Wendell Berry, "Our Deserted Country"

> What is necessary for freedom is not wealth. What is necessary is security and a place of one's own shielded from the claims of the public. What is necessary for the public realm is that it be shielded from the private interests which have intruded upon it in the most brutal and aggressive form.
> —Hannah Arendt, "Public Rights and Private Interests"

In 1963, Hannah Arendt announced " . . . there can only be real democracy . . . where the centralization of power . . . has been broken, and replaced with a diffusion of power into the many power centers of a federal system."[1] Twenty-five years later, Wendell Berry declared that our "place of safety can only be the community, and not just one community, but many of them everywhere."[2] Arendt and Berry share a concern with the need to break up the ever-more massively centralized economic society in which we live in order to establish many shared spaces of public life and freedom. Berry's use of the word "safety" here refers not to a traditional social security apparatus, but rather to what he calls a few lines earlier the "freedom to take care of ourselves and of each other . . . the freedom of community life."[3] Likewise, Arendt sets the breaking up of mass society as a necessary first step toward the "individual taking active responsibility for public affairs."[4] Yet, what would be the nature of this breaking up, and where and how would it take place? What strategies do Arendt and Berry propose to facilitate resistance to our centralized bureaucratic and corporate society?

Berry and Arendt adamantly agree that mass organizations, both private and governmental (and regardless of their stated purpose), represent the chief promoters of this unlivable life. At the same time, neither regards bureaucratic government nor conventional party politics as offering a way to enact change: in effect, neither thinks that we can oppose mass politics with mass resistance. What forms of response are left to us then? How can we significantly alter the world in which we live if we do not organize on a national if not a global scale?

For Arendt, the loss of ownership of a private place in the world is a crucial part of the problem and thus, a possible part of a solution. This expropriation is inherent in both capitalist and socialist superstructures. Berry shares this concern with loss of place in his appeal to the Jeffersonian primacy of the small farm and farmer, but he emphasizes the dislocating efforts of government and corporations in a way that appears more concrete than it does for Arendt. On the other hand, Arendt provides us with a sense of the longer-term historical roots of this expropriation, though her account is largely European in scope. One could argue that they share a core common principle, namely that the only way to effectively resist expropriation—both the loss of private place and the loss of an effective base for public life—is by instituting new forms of "propriation," new ways of finding a place in the world by belonging on a concrete piece of land. Yet, how can small local communities possibly bring about change in the large and complicated world in which we find ourselves? How can the antiquated principle of the primacy of local life possibly solve the many problems of living together in mass consumer society defined by waste economy? The persistence and urgency of these questions only shows the importance of the concerns that they share, particularly to questions pertaining to the political and lived qualities essential to a viable community or commonwealth and to the long history of the loss of land-based community.

I. Commons, Wealth, and Commonwealth

Berry frames the problem of a community of livable scale in terms of the question of commonwealth. His use of this term points to a complex local shared life, one that he pits against the traditional notion of the political body:

> The great enemy of freedom is the alignment of political power with wealth. This alignment destroys the commonwealth—that is, the natural wealth of localities and the local economies of household, neighborhood, and community—and so destroys democracy, of which the commonwealth is the foundation and the political means. This happens—it is happening—because the alignment of wealth and power permits economic value to overturn value of any other kind.[5]

Clearly Berry is not referring to an international, national, or even state commonwealth, such as the Commonwealth of Kentucky. Rather, he appeals to a notion of commonwealth that is more local, more lived, and more livable. Such a commonwealth is built on a "democratic distribution of usable property."[6] Berry argues that the precedent for such a local commonwealth is found in local communities that existed in various parts of the United States as recently as just after the Second World War. These local communities were primarily subsistent, independent, and internally interdependent. Their independence was based on the diversity of their products as well as the mutual dependence of their exchanges. This inherently local economic order was based on a system of exchanges specific to each local commonwealth, where the public life existed in close proximity to the private life of each family.

Arendt's reminder that we live in the wake of a double meaning of commonwealth finds resonance in Berry's more local and earthly account of community. In its original forms, the term "commonwealth" referred more directly to the smaller, more local public good. In fact, the *common weal* was not about conventional wealth first and foremost, but about common wellness that included, but went beyond, the scope of modern economic parameters. In this earliest of modern definitions of commonwealth (or latest of medieval or feudal definitions, depending on how one reckons it), welfare or wellbeing was more than just an accounting of individual financial wealth. However, by 1660, the meaning of commonwealth had undergone a fundamental shift. Commonwealth came to mean the aggregate generation and accumulation of wealth in the state, or as Arendt phrases it, the "common wealth" not the commonweal or common good:

> Common wealth, therefore, can never become common in the sense we speak of a common world; it remained, or rather was intended to remain, strictly private. Only the government, appointed to shield the private owners from each other in the competitive struggle for more wealth, was common.[7]

Thus, the new operating standard, the new priority, was the acquisition of private wealth. Now the commonwealth would be measured by the sum total of national wealth accumulated by individual gentry and merchants (minus the losses produced by various nonproductive groups).[8] The common good was to be calculated primarily in terms of the generation, acquisition, and consumption of goods. Thus, the increasingly central task of the state was to serve as referee in this contest of acquisitive individualism and as a promoter of the productive systems that enable the accumulation of this private and public national wealth. In this way, the path was cleared for securing a national economy as a productive and consumptive commonwealth.

For both Arendt and Berry, this notion of commonwealth as the sum total of individuals producing and competing for distant or abstract wealth skews our understanding of economy. This understanding of economy no longer centers on the activities by which individuals and families support their private homes. Instead, economy is much larger and more concerned with the reality of society. Or to put it in terms that Berry uses in his essay "The Total Economy," the line connecting the myriad local economies to the total economy is broken, thus freeing the total economy from transient considerations such as local subsistence and equity. The larger commonwealth no longer owes anything more than a vague historical debt to local commonwealths. Consequently, the new commonwealth involves a fundamentally different view of how and where people should live, as well as what their primary activities should be, a view that is no longer tethered to the land-based economy. As a means of attempting to imagine alternatives to this dominant reality of the acquisitive and consumptive commonwealth, Berry and Arendt both draw on an early American model, the precedent of the Jeffersonian ward or commons.

II. Placing the Jeffersonian Commons

Perhaps one of the clearest connections between Arendt and Berry is their shared appeal to Jefferson's concept of the ward republics. Both recognize Jefferson's late-in-life call for a vital and dynamic public life at the most local level as a key insight, one that sheds light on the early trajectory of the country as well as our own contemporary crisis of public (and private) life. However, while Arendt is primarily focused on the question of the public life of the wards, Berry is more concerned with the preservation and restoration of local land communities that necessarily depends on this dispersal and broad-based propriation of land. Alongside Jefferson's concern with the formation of the elementary republics is his concern with the dispersal of land to as many small farmers as possible. These two concerns are in fact one for him. With this in mind, one can read Jefferson's appeal to the wards as not so much a theoretical endeavor but rather as a recollection of the local landed communities that served as the inspiration for the constitutional project with its focus on smaller or limited government. However, the fact that states and perhaps even counties come to be the definition of smaller and more self-determining rule by the people shows the loss of the truly local form of public life.

When taken together, Berry and Arendt can help us to understand the complex connections at play in Jefferson's notion of the wards. While this emphasis on possessing (and being possessed by) the land is not an overt theme in Arendt's work, she does offer some hints that suggest this primacy of land-based community is at least implicit in her understanding of what constitutes a viable community. In other words, for both Berry and Arendt what defines our current predicament are the losses of a concrete common world whose viability depends on a belonging to the land as more than an abstract site for occupation. Much of the evidence for this shared problematic of world in Arendt and Berry can be found in their expressed respective debts to the Jeffersonian commons.

If one stops to reflect on Jefferson's account of the wards, it seems hard to imagine that this local grounding of public life could happen without broad-based ownership of the land by all the ward's residents. In other words, the members of the ward must by definition be grounded both in public and in private places. While Arendt does not emphasize it as directly as Berry, she echoes the Jeffersonian call for broad-based disbursement of land quite forcefully in her more contemporary recommendation for how best to resist the forces of expropriation that essentially define her view of the modern world:

> These processes of expropriation you have everywhere. To make a decent amount of property available to every human being—not expropriate, but to spread property—then you will have some possibilities for freedom even under the rather inhuman conditions of modern production.[9]

In pointing to this statement, I am not arguing that Arendt sees the return of land-based community to be as urgent and essential as Berry, but rather that Berry's approach resonates with Arendt's, adding something crucial to her embrace of Jefferson's call for the empowering of the wards. In other words, when read together, they offer us some sense of what such a local emphasis might have made and might still make possible. If somehow enacted or institutionalized, what would the wards do to resurrect the revolutionary spirit, or as Jefferson called it "the spirit of resistance"?[10] Of course, as Arendt points out, we have instead institutionalized the loss of land, both governmentally and socially, both by economic pressures and by individual choice.

How exactly would small and locally based public life enhance the overall public life of our nation? The answer might be found in a consideration of Berry's term, neighborliness. Small public meetings, always ongoing and never fully finished, might bring those who live side by side into productive debate, despite their party affiliations (as opposed to our abstract social media driven "public interactions"). Such meetings would bring those who know one another into repeated discussions that would reveal minor differences of opinion that would not likely show up in larger, more formal, and more constrained, party events. Further, such discussions would be likely to spill over into everyday life, onto street corners and across fence posts. In other words, they would spread spontaneously with little bureaucratic barrier or discouragement (or social media driven "encouragement"). Further, and this may be especially important, the issues that such ward members would be likely to discuss would tend to be local matters, problems close to home and small enough to be effectively addressed and remedied. Neighborliness is most effective in such local arrangements.

I would argue that in Arendt's reading of Jefferson, one finds an account of neighborliness, albeit by another name. For Jefferson, neighbors are more than private connections. They are the public realm writ small because in the meeting of neighbors the private has already become more than private. The public begins with this consistent connection between those who live near one another and share the ambient world of lane and town. If it becomes something more abstract, if this daily or almost daily interaction ceases to be part of the lives of most citizens, then public life is all but lost, for no longer is "the country . . . a living presence in the midst of its citizens."[11] Any attempt to create a sense of community that does not draw from this local public life will be only that, a *sense* of community. Jefferson's assertion of the essential value of the ward life is received as a sort of urgent plea and reminder that this most local form of public life is the germ from which all public reality springs.

Yet, even if such wards became a broad-based working reality, even if such local meetings on local issues became commonplace and widespread, what would this actually do to promote public discourse and exchange at the larger levels of county, state, nation, or globe? How would it help to break down the sclerotic party functioning that seems to have immobilized and paralyzed bona fide public life at these larger levels? Finally, what would this active locality of discourse do to address the "corruption from below" that worries Jefferson, Arendt, and Berry, a corruption of the local that will ultimately lead to the loss of land community as both the private and the public norm in the space of a little more than a century?

The final section of this paper examines the ways in which Jefferson's concern with the corruption of the most local forms of community informs the work of both Arendt and Berry in fundamental ways. By examining their reflections on the nature of this double legacy of local corruption—of land and community—we can better understand how we came to live in a world in which place and belonging are identified almost entirely by our individual wants and needs, that are defined as Berry puts it "by a kind of displaced or placeless citizenship and by commerce with impersonal and self-interested suppliers."[12] It is to the history of this rise of "placeless citizenship" that I want to turn now, a history in which we participate willingly and at least half-knowingly, for the long history of the loss of land-based communities is not a story of necessity but of opportunities taken and exploited, of a largely chosen forgetfulness of most of the losses accompanied by an extreme celebration of many of the gains.

III. "Corruption from Below": Filling in the Long Modern History of the Lost Treasure of Land-Based Community

Arendt's laudatory comments about Jefferson in *On Revolution* are well known. She credits him with an effort to think through the implications, both good and bad, of the fledgling US republic, a republic that he led the way in crafting, and a republic that he knew to be as fragile as its people's determination to maintain it. Arendt offers Jefferson's later obsession with the problem of corruption, both public and private, as evidence of his protective impulses. In her account of Jefferson's worries about the spread of private corruption, or "corruption from below," one finds perhaps the most important connection between Arendt and Berry, namely an effort on both their parts to trace elements of the long history by which ever-growing economic commitments come to all but bury the possibility of a broad-based and locally centered public life. Read together, Berry and Arendt offer us a different way of understanding how we have come to live in a world whose chief virtues are expropriation and consumption, virtues that have been willingly embraced despite their costs to both the people and the land.

Consider this passage from *On Revolution* which comes near the end of Arendt's extensive reflections on Jefferson's concerns about private corruption and the lost treasure of public life in the new republic:

> However, under conditions, not of prosperity as such, but of rapid and constant economic growth, that is, of a constantly increasing expansion of the private realm—and these were of course the conditions of the modern age—the dangers of corruption and perversion were much more likely to arise from private interests than from public power. And it speaks for the high caliber of Jefferson's statesmanship that he was able to perceive this danger despite his preoccupation with the older and better-known threats of corruption in bodies politic.[13]

Arendt attributes her account of Jefferson's worry about the growth of a pervasive private corruption to issues that she herself raises about the birth of the modern age, say in something like 17th-century England. But she also points to matters that will not fully arise until at least 50 to 100 years after Jefferson's death. Thus, Arendt challenges us to think through a type of long history that both precedes and follows the moment in which the possibility of widespread local public life in the early U.S. republic was still at least imaginable, if not attainable. In crude historical terms, the span of time with which Arendt's history of expropriation is concerned is at least 300–400 years. To make matters more challenging, we are obliged to recognize that this history can only be properly thought through in terms of changes in specific nations (e.g., the loss of the commons in 16th- and 17th-century England, the rise of industrialism in late 18th- and early 19th-century England, etc.). Arendt's focus on the early United States in *On Revolution* is helpful and clarifying in this respect, but the ambivalent connection between Colonial America and England means we are confronted by a much more complicated story, one that needs to be thoroughly explored if we are to understand issues such as the commodification of land, the loss of place as a basic political principle, and so forth. This is what I am calling the long modern history of the lost treasure of land-based community. However, to make this long history more visible and more credible, let's turn to Wendell Berry's concept of total economy

In an essay by the same name, Berry defines total economy as "an unrestrained taking of profits from the disintegration of nations, communities, households, landscapes, and ecosystems. It licenses symbolic or artificial wealth to 'grow' by means of the destruction of the real wealth of the world."[14] One can ask, when did this total economy first arise, when did it begin to show itself, and how was it born? In other words, even though what Berry terms "total economy" is clearly meant as an indictment of the contemporary dominance of corporate and governmental operations, where "state and national governments . . . begin to act as agents of the global economy," he offers a hint concerning the genealogy of this total economy when he writes that "significant and sometimes critical choices that once belonged to individuals and communities [have] become the property of corporations."[15]

Berry gives us an even clearer sense of the standard of life prior to the rise of total economy in his reference to Jefferson in his *The Unsettling of America* where he writes that the bonds between people and land "are not merely those of economics and property, but those, at once more feeling and more practical, that comes from the investment in a place and a community of work, devotion, knowledge, memory, and association."[16] The gap between what Berry calls "local economy" and "total economy" lies in the fact that life prior to the rise of total economy was (and still is in a relatively few small places!) not dominated by matters solely of economy and saleable property, but rather by a broader and deeper sense of connection between people and between them and the land on which they lived. As Berry puts it in his Jefferson Lecture, lived economy "refers to the husbanding of all the goods by which we live. An authentic economy, if we had one, would define and make, on the terms of thrift and affection, our connections to nature and one another. Our present industrial system also makes those connections, but by pillage and indifference."[17] Total economy, the fullest form of industrial economy to date, has thus removed local structural encumbrances in favor of a more efficient system of production, consumption, and waste. Or as Berry puts it, to "be a consumer in the total economy, one must agree to be totally ignorant, totally passive, and totally dependent on distant supplies and self-interested suppliers."[18]

Of course, what Berry is describing by total economy bears directly on Arendt's account of consumer society in Section 17 of *The Human Condition*. The term she will use at the very end of that section (i.e., the end of the Labor chapter) is "waste economy." In the culmination of her account of "A Consumers' Society" she declares that "our whole economy has become a waste economy, in which things must be almost as quickly devoured and discarded as they have appeared in the world, if the process itself is not to come to a catastrophic end."[19] Arendt will expand on this idea of the waste economy in the first section of the last chapter of *The Human Condition,* where she states that under "modern conditions, not destruction but conservation spells ruin."

This entire passage, both prior to and as a follow up to her description of waste economy in the Germany of the late 1940s and early 1950s is couched in an assessment of the grave and chronic dangers (and "virtues") of the long story of expropriation, a story that stretches by her own historical clues from the 1550s to the 1950s. There is little doubt that Arendt recognizes that the loss of land-based community is at the heart of this long history of expropriation as evidenced by her assertion that "expropriation and world alienation coincide, and the modern age, very much against the intentions of all the actors in the play, began with by alienating certain elements of the population from the world."[20] On the same page of the introduction to the last chapter of *The Human Condition* Arendt offers a direct anticipation of her reflection on the Jeffersonian commons in the last chapter of *On Revolution*. She states that "property . . . indicates the privately owned share of a common world . . . [and] is the most elementary political condition for man's worldliness."[21] Thus, when read against the backdrop of Berry's concern, as well as her own work in *On Revolution*, *The Human Condition*, and *The Origins of Totalitarianism*, Arendt's account of the rise of consumer society contributes yet another segment of the long history of the loss of land-based community, albeit without the explicit and direct emphasis that Berry places on the connection between the common well-being of the land and its people. Consider the following passage from Berry's 2012 NEH address, a passage that shines light on the question of corruption from below by way of broad-based responsibility for the global industrial economy as the latest installment in the saga of the loss of land-based community:

> That we live now in an economy that is not sustainable is not the fault only of a few mongers of power and heavy equipment. We all are implicated. We all, in the course of our daily economic life, consent to it, whether or not we approve of it. This is because of the increasing abstraction and unconsciousness of our connection to our economic sources in the land, the land-communities, and the land-use economies.[22]

Compare this quote to Arendt's own admonishment of the postwar willingness to equate the business of freedom with the business of business:

> When we were told that by freedom we understood free enterprise, we did very little to dispel this monstrous falsehood, and all too often we have acted as though we too believed that it was wealth and abundance which were at stake. . . .[23]

Berry and Arendt both connect the rise of the industrial economy with the complicity of all of us as consumers and the embrace of abstract global economic principles to justify our participation. In their respective readings,

Arendt and Berry show the ways in which Jefferson's worry with "corruption from below" reaches a full yet largely silent accomplishment with the rise of mid- to late 20th-century consumer society. This is not to suggest Jefferson possessed some extraordinary prescience but serves only to point to the dynamic that concerned Jefferson, namely that without an ongoing connection to a local public life citizens will cease to be citizens and become private individuals concerned almost solely with the protection of their private rights. This loss of public life by lack of use and lack of connection, the withering away of impulses such as public spirit and public happiness, is the moral that Arendt draws from Jefferson's worries over the loss of the local commons:

> What remained of them in America, after the revolutionary spirit had been forgotten, were civil liberties, the individual welfare of the greatest number, and public opinion as the greatest force ruling an egalitarian, democratic society. This transformation corresponds with great precision to the invasion of the public realm by society; it is as though the originally political principles were translated into social values.[24]

This passage occurs prior to Arendt's discussion of Jefferson's concern of the "mortal danger" that arose when all the power had been given to the people, "without giving them the opportunity of *being* republicans and of *acting* like citizens."[25] Nonetheless, this translation and transformation of public principles into social values is facilitated by this lack of public life and by the absence of a place where local public life can flourish. In short, one can draw a clear line of legacy between the loss of a shared and landed life beyond the countless private lives of wealth acquisition and the eventual acceptance of this fact as a social value. The corruption from below that so worried Jefferson becomes the social norm once the revolutionary spirit which was so grounded in landed community has become a distant cultural memory.

By way of conclusion, I want to turn to the question of Berry and Arendt's respective appeals to imagination as a necessary step in undoing this public forgetfulness of the lost treasure of land-based community.

Conclusion: Local Affection and Amor Mundi: Historical Imagination and the Resistance of Belonging to the Land

While the consequences of ignorance, oblivion, and failure to remember are conspicuous and of a simple, elementary nature, the same is not true of the historical processes which brought all this about.[26] I have been describing an enormous failure, and to me this appears to be a failure of imagination. Though we are now far advanced in the destruction of our country, we have only begun to imagine what our country is. We are destroying it *because* of our failure to imagine it. By *imagination* I do not mean the ability to make things up or to make a realistic copy. I mean the ability to make real to oneself the life of one's place or the life of an enemy-and therein, I believe, is implied, imagination in the highest sense.[27]

For both Arendt and Berry our complicity in the formation of the long history of the loss of land-based community hinges on the question of a failure to remember and a failure of imagination. To address the problem of our long-standing tradition of joint participation in this corruption from below, let's return to the question of the commonwealth as a new set of possibilities, but guided by the grounded past as the basis for our deliberations. Arendt's account of the damaged, self-defeating, commonwealth of, for example, 17th-century England can be read not simply as a statement of fact but also as historical guidance for the beginning of this loss of a common shared life.[28] In other words, she offers it as a negative imaginative model. We could thus begin by reflecting on the older notion of the commons, a notion that Jefferson seems to have borrowed in his concept of the wards. Perhaps we have forgotten what so many of the founding fathers and mothers took for granted, namely that land, both shared and disbursed, may be the only proper site for both our private and joint lives. Perhaps our forgetfulness, though productive, stems from our unwillingness to imagine other possibilities besides those insisted upon by modern mass consumeristic society.

One of the key concerns that Arendt and Berry share is that we must stop using the dominant forms of social and economic thinking as our sometimes stark, but often shrouded, guidelines for political and personal life. Arendt's pursuit of the question of the social, both in terms of the rise of the social realm, as well as in her concern with the dominance of the social question in the revolutionary tradition, represent efforts to show the ways in which social and economic theory represent efforts to legitimize placelessness and political impotence and isolation. Berry's criticism of a modern agricultural science dominated by industrial economic principles and practices offers a way of grounding and extending Arendt's concerns with the hegemony of socio-economic thinking. In short, such thinking and the practices which are guided by it have served to efface a double question, namely; where do we belong and with whom? And, if this is the case, what other means besides theoretical reflection could possibly serve as an alternative?

Rather than overdependence on theoretical systems, both Arendt and Berry appeal to a different, less structured, form of understanding, namely imagination. This shared reliance on imagination as the chief form of interrogation and understanding stems from their distinct but resonant efforts to remember both the better and the worst in our historical legacy in terms of where we now stand. It is not a question of returning to a simpler time, but of confronting the reality of our alienated communities in terms of what might be. Arendt and Berry's accounts represent a clue to understanding the importance of historical and political imagination for reconsidering the loss of our sense of place. According to Berry, there is a very old precedent for pursuing this link between imagination and belonging:

> I will say, from my own belief and experience, that imagination thrives on contact, on tangible connection. For humans to have a responsible relationship to the world, they must imagine their places in it. To have a place, to live and belong in a place, to live from a place without destroying it, we must imagine it. By imagination we see it illuminated by its own unique character and by our love for it. By imagination we recognize with sympathy the fellow members, human and nonhuman, with whom we share our place. By that local experience we see the need to grant a sort of preemptive sympathy to all the fellow members, the neighbors, with whom we share the world. As imagination enables sympathy, sympathy enables affection. And it is in affection that we find the possibility of a neighborly, kind, and conserving economy.[29]

Berry's account sheds new light on what Arendt terms the "American failure to remember," providing the opportunity to see it as more than simply a conceptual loss but also a loss of place, or the loss of the sustaining meaning of land. This seems inherent in Jefferson's use of political imagination to summon the power and value of the wards, as both Berry and Arendt read it. In fact, Arendt says as much at the beginning of Chapter 5 of *On Revolution*, although she couches it in terms of property rather than land:

> We have difficulties today in perceiving the great potency of this principle because the intimate connection between property and freedom is for us no longer a matter of course. . . . Not before the 20th century were people exposed directly and without any personal protection to the pressures of either state or society; and only when people emerged who were free without owning property to protect their liberties were laws necessary to protect persons and personal freedom directly, instead of merely protecting their property.[30]

If we read this passage as an effort to remember what has been lost (as well as what has been gained) then we can better understand the way in which modern civil liberties represent only a partial substitute for the way in which private land and public space once combined to ground a more effective (and in Berry's words, more affective) community. Or to put it more bluntly, between Berry and Arendt we can trace the texture of our long-term joint participation in the loss of place, private and public. The rise of the new norm of placelessness, of expropriation as a social virtue, has been fueled by the ongoing mass acceptance of abstract individual rights as a surrogate for power, the power that comes "into being where people get together and bind themselves through promises, covenants, and mutual pledges," particularly where this coming together is understood concretely and not in some abstract way.[31]

Perhaps it will be argued that I have pushed Arendt too far in the direction of Berry. Surely, she would not claim as he does that the fate of the land and the fate of the people are one and the same? And yet if we return to her last comments on Jefferson in *On Revolution,* we find the following passage by way of her summary of Jefferson's late-in-life political reflections:

> When, at the end of his life, he summed up what to him clearly was the gist of private and public morality, "Love your neighbor as yourself, and your country more than yourself," he knew that this maxim remained an empty exhortation unless the "country" could be made as present to the "love" of its citizens as the "neighbor" was to the love of his fellow men. For just as there could not be much substance to the neighborly love if one's neighbor should make a brief appearance once every two years, so there could not be much substance to the admonition to love one's country more than oneself unless the country was a living presence in the midst of its citizens.[32]

Try as I might to bracket what Berry has to say on the relation of people and land, and of course much of what he has to say is greatly influenced by Jefferson's views, I find it hard to read what Arendt offers here as not about love of the country as love of land. How else can one understand what she means by the "substance" and the "living presence" of the country as not necessarily including love of land, soil, place, and earth? And how are we to understand the importance of the living presence of other people if not on the land that we share, both as private abode and as public place?

• • •

I fear that it will take a long time for us to familiarize ourselves with such a sense of shared place grounded in the land. Until we do, however, I suspect we will always be bereft of that sense of belonging that may, in fact, only arise when people know each other intimately and well because they live in the same locale sharing on a daily basis a sense of appreciation for the place in which they jointly live. The beauty of modern mass society is that we are relieved (truly relieved) of such intimate knowledge. I already know what you want and need because it must surely be precisely what I (and everybody else) want and need. I don't need to talk with or listen and you don't have to risk sharing your wants and needs with me. Or we may share these wants and needs and little more when we happen to interact.

Such local belonging would seem to distract us from our most important activities, and the trivial work inherent in such belonging to land and the people who live on the land near us will strike us as tiresome, restrictive, and banal. Of course, this is because we are already bored by the grave limits that our social and economic liberties have placed on our capacity for imagining another way of living. Once one has begun to receive everything that one could possibly want, it is hard to imagine any other way to live. The abundant society blinds us to the possibilities of a life not defined so narrowly, a life that would favor thrift and collaborative work over waste and a pervasive sense of limited even suspended responsibility. Through our liberated eyes, living "savingly" seems instead like a restriction of the truly free life.

We will have to work hard together to remember how we got here. We will have to work very hard to remember the losses as well as the gains, and the choices that we, our parents, and their parents have made, and why we made them. We will have to imagine how it might have been different, and then question just how far our imagination has gone (or just how far gone our imagination is!). Worldliness depends on our being at home with others. The question is whether we can be at home in a place with more than the 100 or the 300 that Jefferson imagines. For all our intellectual, social, and technological advancements it is not clear that we can truly belong in a place with more than a small community of people. And, of course, these people must make it their first and abiding concern to care for the place in which they live and the people with whom they share this place. In this way, affection for the land and love of the world meet to provide a home for those who care enough to be placed rather than placeless. It is here that the resistance of belonging overcomes the refusal, both passive and active, to share the world with others in more than an abstract manner.

But how can this localization of public life take place in the midst of our increasingly mass society? This may be the most difficult question we face because it will require us to reconsider choices and decisions that are not simply our own, choices and decisions that were made before we arrived and after we came of age. In other words, we will have to accept our responsibility not only for our actions and choices but also for those made before we were born. However, before we can accept this expanded responsibility, we must understand what it is we are taking on. Let us begin by recognizing that such a beginning cannot be generalized. Arendt's account of the singularity of the US revolution implies that such breaking cannot be repeatable or generalizable. It is not a question of simply undoing hundreds of years of centralizing and social dependency. We must begin again in a thousand or million cases, each an event all its own. In other words, the mass replication that got us into this mess, this theoretical multiplication of neutralized action cannot simply be unraveled. Perhaps as Merleau-Ponty once said, we must reweave the web that defines our public and private lives. This can only be done on a case by case, township by township, village by village, parish by parish, canton by canton basis.

Why is this localization not simply repeatable? According to Berry, it is because the reasons why we choose a place, perhaps despite the people, or why we choose the people, perhaps despite the place, turns on taste and affection. For most of us this means extricating ourselves from placelessness by becoming part of a place but a place that is something more than an abstract site that can be replaced at any given moment. In this effort, we would do well to reflect on Wendell's good fortune and Arendt's resilience. Thus, it is not theory but affection and will embodied in countless small places that will help us move, but only in the context of neighborliness and shared imagination, and the "incessant talk" that embodies these small virtues.

If as Arendt warns we must learn to think without banisters, then we may also surely have to act without them. However, the risk of walking down these plural paths surely means taking up the question of living in the world jointly and because such joint living is best done—or rather may only be possible—on common ground, we must accept the limitation of a shared place where each can find the affection and obligation to care for what should own us more than we can dispose of it. Thus, to love the world must mean to love our place in it, both as home for each but also as home for all.

I began this paper with a quote from Arendt's 1963 radio address about the breaking up of modern mass society. Of course, those of you who have read the end of *On Revolution* will recognize the language, because she says something similar there as well. Summoning Jefferson one last time in her closing argument on freedom as tangible reality she writes:

> It would be tempting to spin out further the potentialities of the councils, but it certainly is wiser to say with Jefferson, 'Begin them only for a single purpose, they will soon show for what others they are the best instruments'—the best instruments, for example, for breaking up modern mass society, with its dangerous tendency toward the formation of pseudo-political mass movements, or rather, the best the most natural way for interspersing it at the grass roots with an "elite" that is chosen by no one but constitutes itself.[33]

Arendt shares Jefferson's optimistic imagining of what people can do in small groups to safeguard the fullest possibilities of life, both private and public. Her optimism is all the more remarkable because between Jefferson and Arendt lies the fuller unfolding of countless events that comprise the history of the loss of place and the widespread mass participation in so many forms of expropriation that Jefferson could not possibly have foreseen. In any case, it is remarkable to see Arendt once again summon the power of grassroots organization, of small local meetings of the people, even in the face of the many forms of complicity by which the "corruption from below" has "perverted all virtues into social values."[34] This is the merit and the folly of political imagination, to know that what has happened never fully defines what might be possible. Such a shared imagination helps us to recognize that the social and economic systems that seem to have trapped us once and for all are only as foolproof as our complicity makes them, and that the way out is not through mimicking those vast systems in our efforts to undo them but rather in returning to the smallest of all possible solutions, to ask our neighbors and ourselves what we should be doing today. After all, where else can the grassroots possibly grow if not on this land of and between our homes? It is there in the smallest and most local places that the possibilities of renewal and new beginning can be fostered by the incessant talk of those who care about such matters and those who actively love the places that serve as the stage for this unending conversation and accompanying actions. Perhaps only in such local events can consent and approval authentically coincide.

Bibliography

Agar, Herbert and Allen Tate, eds. *Who Owns America? A New Declaration of Independence* (Wilmington, Delaware: ISI Books, 1999).

Arendt, Hannah, *Between Past and Future: Eight Exercises in Political Thought* (New York: Penguin, 2006).

Arendt, Hannah, *Essays in Understanding: 1930-1954* (New York: Schocken, 1994).

Arendt, Hannah, *On Revolution* (New York: Penguin, 2006).

Arendt, Hannah, *The Human Condition* (Chicago: Chicago University Press, 1998).

Arendt, Hannah, *The Origins of Totalitarianism* (New York: Schocken, 2004).

Arendt, Hannah, "Hannah Arendt on Hannah Arendt," In *Thinking Without a Banister: Essays in Understanding 1953-1975*, edited by Jerome Kohn, pp. 443-475 (New York: Schocken, 2018).

Arendt, Hannah, *The Promise of Politics* (New York: Schocken, 2005).

Arendt, Hannah, "Nation-State and Democracy," *Arendt Studies* 1 (2017): pp. 7-12. https doi: 10.5840/arendtstudies20171

Arendt, Hannah, "Public Rights and Private Interests: A Response to Charles Frankel." In *Thinking Without a Banister: Essays in Understanding 1953-1975*, edited by Jerome Kohn, pp. 506-512 (New York: Schocken, 2018).

Barry, James, "The Growth of the Social in Arendt's Post-Mortem of the Nation-State," *Telos* 138 (2007): pp. 97-119.

Berry, Wendell, *Citizenship Papers* (Berkeley: Counterpoint, 2014).

Berry, Wendell, *The Hidden Wound* (Berkeley: Counterpoint, 2010).

Berry, Wendell, *Home Economics* (San Francisco: Northpoint Press, 1987).

Berry, Wendell, *It All Turns on Affection: The Jefferson Lecture and Other Essays.* (Berkeley: Counterpoint, 2012).

Berry, Wendell, *The Long-Legged House* (Berkeley: Counterpoint, 2012).

Berry, Wendell, *Our Only World* (Berkeley: Counterpoint, 2015).

Berry, Wendell, *The Unsettling of America: Culture and Agriculture* (Berkeley: Counterpoint, 2015).

Berry, Wendell, "American Imagination and the Civil War," *The Sewanee Review*, Vol. 115, No. 4 (Fall, 2007), pp. 587–602.

I'll Take My Stand: The South and the Agrarian Tradition (Baton Rouge: Louisiana State University Press, 1977).

Neeson, J. M., *Commoners: Common Right, Enclosure and Social Change in England, 1700-1820.* (Cambridge: Cambridge University Press, 1993).
Wendell Berry and Ellen Davis, "The Art of Being Creatures," Interview by Krista Tippett, *On Being with Krista Tippett*, June 20, 2010. onbeing.org/programs/wendell-berry-ellen-davis-the-art-of-being-creatures/#transcript

Notes

1. Hannah Arendt, "Nation-State and Democracy," Arendt Studies 1, p. 12.
2. Wendell Berry, *The Hidden Wound*, p. 129.
3. Berry, *The Hidden Wound*, p. 129.
4. Arendt, "Nation-State and Democracy," p. 12.
5. Berry, *Hidden Wound*, p. 127. This passage is from the 1988 Afterword.
6. Berry, *The Unsettling of America*, p. xi.
7. Arendt, *The Human Condition*, p. 69.
8. See J. M. Neeson's *Commoners*, p. 298.
9. "Hannah Arendt on Hannah Arendt," in *Thinking Without a Banister: Essays in Understanding* 1953–1975, p. 459.
10. This quote from a letter to Abigail Adams is in keeping with Jefferson's "tree of liberty" quote which was found in a letter written several months later (to William Smith).
11. Arendt, *On Revolution*, p. 245.
12. Berry, *The Hidden Wound*, pp. 126–7.
13. *On Revolution*, p. 244.
14. Berry, *Citizenship Papers*, p. 72.
15. Ibid.
16. Berry, *The Unsettling of America*, p. 147.
17. Berry, "Jefferson Lecture," p. 6?
18. Berry, Citizenship Papers, p. 74. It is worth noting that Berry repeats the term "self-interested suppliers," a phrase he used in both his 1988 Afterword to The Hidden Wound in his 2000 essay, "The Total Economy."
19. Arendt, *The Human Condition*, p. 134.
20. Arendt, *The Human Condition*, p. 253.
21. Arendt, *The Human Condition*, p. 253. Also, see the footnote at the bottom of p. 253 where she anticipates Berry's idea of total economy by defining prosperity in terms of goods produced to be wasted and used up in destruction.
22. Wendell Berry, "2012 Jefferson Lecture," p. 7.
23. Arendt, *On Revolution*, p. 209.
24. Arendt, *On Revolution*, p. 213.
25. Arendt, *On Revolution*, p. 245.
26. Arendt, *On Revolution*, p. 210.
27. Berry, "American Imagination and the Civil War," pp. 596–7.
28. Notice that this critical account of the commonwealth is found at the beginning of the section entitled "The Social and the Private." Arendt's account of the invasion of the social figures prominently in the last chapter of On Revolution as well as in The Human Condition.
29. Berry, It All Turns on Affection, p. 14.
30. Arendt, *On Revolution*, p. 172.
31. Arendt, On Revolution, p. 172. See pp. 209–213 for Arendt's extended account of the "failure to remember" and the "failure to understand" that seem to be an essential aspect of this substitution of social rights for place.
32. Arendt, *On Revolution*, p. 245.
33. Arendt, *On Revolution*, p. 271.
34. Arendt, *On Revolution*, p. 268.

Learning our Native Tongue: America as a Project

Tracy B. Strong

I have three claims: The first is a general claim, and it's that any revitalization of any given democracy must or will have to draw upon the spirit, the *Geist*, the *esprit*—as in Montesquieu, Nietzsche, de Tocqueville—of that particular country.

My second, more restricted, claim is that the experiences of Americans over their history do themselves provide the bases for a revitalization of our American democracy. Notice, by the way, that I'm using the word "American" a lot. We've been, I think, less than country-specific here, even though we've talked about countries. It is the case our own history might provide the basis for revitalization. It is also the case that our historical oblivion is such that these particular bases are mostly ignored. However, at various moments in our history they have been available, only generally to be swept under by contingencies and what used to be called "the interests."

And lastly, because of this, America has always been a project. As Langston Hughes wrote in 1935, "Oh, let America be America again—/ The land that never yet has been yet—/ And yet must be—the land where *every* man is free."[1]

My title is from a late poem by Robert Frost, "A Cabin in the Clearing."

> **Smoke**
> They must by now have learned the native tongue.
> Why don't they ask the Red Man where they are?
> **Mist**
> They often do, and none the wiser for it.
> So do they also ask philosophers
> Who come to look in on them from the pulpit.
> They will ask anyone there is to ask -
> ...
> Learning has been a part of their religion.[2]

"Learning has been part of their religion." This is our project. From this, I have three themes: First, American democracy is a project always needing to be realized and is thus what Sheldon Wolin called "fugitive." Our crisis is not so much the crisis of democracy; it is the crisis of foregoing or forgetting the project.

Secondly, what being an American citizen entails passes from something individually attained to something collective.

And a third theme: when thought of as collective, citizenship often comes to be thought as something that can be given, thus as a perhaps nonspecifically merited *right*.

Now, what it means to be a citizen can be lost. Losing track of oneself as a citizen is as old as the history of political thought. Take the opening of Socrates's speech in *The Apology*, his defense:

> **Socrates**: [These are the first lines.] How you, oh men of Athens, have been affected by my accusers I do not know, but I for my part almost forgot my own identity, so persuasively did they talk. And yet there's hardly a word of truth in what they have said. [3]

Socrates, at the beginning of political thinking, finds that he's in danger of losing track of what actually being a citizen, an Athenian citizen, means. And from whence might he recall himself? This problem of recollection is our problem, and I think there are three stages to our situation.

The starting point is to understand that even before there was a United States—the term "American" is apparently first used in 1648—Americans struggled over what constituted the adequate signs of the qualities necessary to be called a citizen and call oneself a citizen, that is, for electing and being elected. Citizenship is thus originally not primarily understood as a right, but as the acquiring of certain publicly recognizable virtues that permit one to act and be recognized as a citizen. In that sense, it is not originally a right.

For John Winthrop and John Cotton, these signs, these criteria, were those of Christian virtue as manifest in and entailed by what were the relatively relaxed requirements of church membership, a position that was, in fact, challenged by Roger Williams. If you are a democrat, I would argue you should prefer Winthrop to Williams. Admission to church membership—the criteria were not severe—was therefore the sign that one was a responsible enough person to be entrusted with the serious business of the political realm.

Now, this notion of the visible signs of virtue, of purity—they were the Puritans after all—necessarily changes as time passes, first, during the First Great Awakening, 1730s and '40s, and in particular by the work of ministers like the theologian-scientist Jonathan Edwards, later president of Princeton; Samuel Davies, and others. Edwards and the others recognized and saw the need to deal with the erosion, even disappearance, of the original purity, the manifestation of which had been the original criteria for citizenship—the original purity that had led Englishmen to leave their home and come across the sea.

And here it's worth noting that the problem of this loss of original motivating virtue is identified not only by Edwards—"Sinners in the Hands of an Angry God" is his great sermon—but is still understood as a problem a century later by Hawthorne in *The Scarlet Letter. The Scarlet Letter* is set in the 1640s, and at one point Hawthorne notes that the Puritan children—that is, not the original generation, but the generation which could not have that original purity—the Puritan children amused themselves by—and I'm quoting Hawthorne—"scourging Quakers, taking the scalps from Indians, scaring one another with freak of imitative witchcraft, and finally, by playing at going to church." Such did not bode well.

As Puritan purity was fast fading, the revivalists thought to awaken an intense, positive, fear-based emotion towards virtue so as to revitalize the saliency of church membership: All are "sinners in the hands of an angry God" and the fear of damnation should lead one to focus on virtuous behavior. In the border states such congregations came to include African Americans and women. Whitfield opened his meetings to all, a first step toward universalis: in these meetings no pews were reserved for the rich.

The white population in 1650 is about 50,000; by 1770, it's over two million. The intensity of emotion which Edwards and the others demanded proved difficult to require. In fact, several citizens of Northampton committed suicide in despair. Edwards was fired from his pulpit.

A new grounding for citizenship comes in what one might call gentry republicanism as exemplified by James Madison's early requirement of land ownership for active citizenship (he had a large plantation and numerous slaves). The requirement of land ownership is not so much the manifestation of an ideology favoring the rich—though it has that effect—as it is the claim that land ownership gives those owners a responsibility stake in their country, and thus makes for virtue and reduces the possibility of corruption.

Such a view, however, is soon inadequate to deal with the increasingly large number of unpropertied but literate and self-sufficient artisans, mainly in the cities. By 1780, literacy in New England is about 90 percent. Think here of someone like the silversmith, Paul Revere. To deal with this new issue of urban artisans, Thomas Paine argues that the possession of tools was a sufficient sign for the possibility of virtuous citizenship; this is called democratic republicanism. Producing the means of one's life by one's own hands becomes the criterion entitling participation. We still speak of "tools of the trade," and the tools of one's profession are tax deductible. Jefferson had already observed in 1867 that a lawyer without his books was like a worker without his tools.

By 1850, the US population is 24 million, an increase of one-third from only 1840. A larger scale of citizenship is needed. And the vision of citizenship is again modified, this time, by the individual perfectionism of the Second Great Awakening, and most importantly, by Lincoln. Lincoln gives a great speech to the Temperance Union—he's quite young at this point. As you might expect he makes an argument against alcohol—it's the Temperance Union, after all. What is his argument against alcohol? It's not that booze is a sin, he thinks it's stupid to argue that. He says the problem with alcohol is it makes you lose control, and if you lose control, you're a bad citizen: temperance is a *political* virtue. Lincoln's support of the Free Soil Movement rests on a vision of the self-controlled independent and responsible citizen. To be self-controlled is not to be dependent, not to be a slave.

In 1838, he gives a lecture entitled "The Perpetuation of Our Political Institutions," in which he explores the same problem we've been pursuing: the revolutionary generation had what Lincoln called "a living history," which informed them politically. One knew someone who had fought, someone who was wounded. There were marks on those who went through the Revolutionary War that provided a touchstone for one's sense of who one was as a citizen: a living history. But with time this has faded, and Lincoln seeks to replace it with a new living history. I'm quoting here [Lincoln's Lyceum Address]: "They were the pillars of the temple of liberty, and now that they have crumbled away that temple must fall unless we, their descendants, supply their places with other pillars."[4] It's a brilliant understanding, but it is going to suffer under the economic development of capitalism post–Civil War.

In 1862, Lincoln signs the Homestead Act that gives citizens, future citizens, women, and freed slaves up to 160 acres of public land each, providing they live on it and work it. Nearly 10 percent of the territory of the United States is given away free to over one-and-a-half million individuals. It is this understanding of Lincoln—of the self-controlled, self-sufficient and responsible citizen—that is relevant to a correct understanding of his hostility to slavery.

Lincoln argues that owning slaves made one slavish—a thought, by the way, already found in Rousseau. Always there was a fear of slavery, and not only of chattel slavery. To take an aside here, the *defense* of chattel slavery, as an institution in the South, is ironically made in the name of republican virtue. Southerners like Calhoun and Fitzhugh argued that virtuous citizenship depends on the institution of chattel slavery because it was the only way for the polity to deal adequately with those whom they think cannot be independent, that is, cannot meet the criteria for virtuous citizenship. These, of course, were the slaves: they were deemed like children. The Black population of the United States in 1860 is almost four-and-a-half million, of which four million are enslaved. In this context, the Southerners point to the advantages of a system they call "Christian trusteeship"—taking care of the "children," as it were. They claim, not without some partial plausibility, that chattel slavery has advantages for the slave over the "wage slavery"—notice the slavery metaphor again—that is found in the North. After all, slaves cannot be fired in an economic downturn. Theirs is not centrally an economic argument; it's a criterion argument, though others do make the economic argument.

Slavery is in fact the predominant metaphor for all that is not of the citizen. The fear of slavery arises in other realms, particularly in the nascent feminist movement, where some proclaim marriage to be slavery, as one can't get out of it once in it; thus, there is a lot of argument in favor of divorce in the feminist movement. The feminist movement is important, by the way, not only because it's often associated with the abolitionists, but even more because it provided training in public leadership to a wide range of middle- and upper-middle-class white women, thus preparing an expectation of participation, which, of course, will only be ratified in 1919 by a margin of one vote in the state house of Tennessee.

It's important to note here, though, that these Lincolnian criteria of citizenship—free, independent, able to enjoy the fruits of their own labor—were shared by the newly freed Blacks who claimed citizenship on the same individual grounds as had Lincoln and the others. There is here a not generally known interesting historical fact. After the Civil War, General Sherman, who was a racist, but hated rebels more than he hated Blacks, gives 400,000 acres of good land to newly freed Blacks. The Congress ratifies his grant, but Andrew Johnson, now president, backed inter alia by the *New York Times* and Northern forces, vetoes it. This gives rise to a set of extraordinary documents in which the Blacks petition again and again not to have their land taken away from them. The argument they make for retaining their land is that they worked it. Everything that was produced, they produced, and they are—this is Lincolnianism—entitled to the fruits of their own labors, and no one should be able to take those away from them.

However, Blacks (and women) are nonenfranchised—we are right at the end of the war: they are thus not fully citizens. As such, they form a group, and a major politically important consequence of the Civil War is that it raises the question of the *collective* attainment of citizenship for the newly freed Blacks. Similarly, the question of collective attainment of citizenship for women will be raised by the feminist movement. So, in other words, suddenly after the Civil War, there is a large number of newly freed individuals from slavery. What is to be done? And the answer to that, of course, is the Fourteenth Amendment, not so much the Thirteenth that bars slavery, though that was important. But the Fourteenth Amendment does something new, and it's important to realize what it does. The Fourteenth Amendment *gives* voting citizenship to Blacks and to all who've been born in the United States. Citizenship is now possible as a collective grant, not an individually achieved situation. Sherman himself said that "the hand that picks up the musket cannot be denied the ballot."[5] There is, on Boston Common, a monument to the Black troops that forms the basis for a great poem by Robert Lowell, "For the Union Dead." You may have seen the film *Glory,* which tells the story of the Black troops. Lowell: "[A]t the dedication,/ William James could almost hear the bronze Negroes breathe./ Their monument sticks like a fish bone / in the city's throat."[6] It's a glorious poem, and picks up the whole story of Shaw and his Black regiment. There is a complex and to our day unresolved tension between the bright individualism implicit in Lincoln's thought and the recognition that some problems can only admit of collective solutions. The work of James Baldwin, W. E. B. DuBois, and Malcom X is very clear about this.

With this, we're moving into the post–Civil War, the last quarter or last third of the century. It's an era of unprecedented concentrated wealth and power, of unprecedented inequalities. It is also an era—and here I can't develop the argument—in which the vision of individual self-sufficient citizenship which has evolved presents no necessary conflict with the economic developments.

We are into the Gilded Age, an age of gross inequalities. Blacks can now vote but with the end of reconstruction, they are increasingly kept from it in the South (and would remain so for almost one hundred years). Across the country, inequalities are great and manifest, but they are importantly resisted across the board by the lower and working classes. There are over 42,000 strikes between 1870 and 1900. Their cartoons depict, for instance, Standard Oil as a monopoly octopus with its tentacles out; or the House chamber with the fat cats of the trusts sitting behind the congressmen whom they own and control—there are many of these cartoons. One of my favorites, in a journal called *Puck,* which was published in both German and English, depicts the snake of monopoly with its coils around the Capitol threatening Ms. Liberty. And little Puck over on the side is saying to Uncle Sam, "Well, what are you going to do about it?" This kind of resistance, this kind of movement, is extremely widespread, and it manifests itself again and again.

Prior to the Civil War, the United States was only partly a capitalist nation. Economic changes had produced these unprecedented concentrations of wealth, completely unregulated, by the way. A number of movements did grow up in response, which were individually focused, economically radical. One thinks of the Knights of Labor, the Grange, the Greenbackers, and others. Two groups will eventually be the most important among these: the Populists and Socialists. Two figures dominate here: William Jennings Bryan, in 1896, the Democratic/Populist candidate for president following his great "Cross of Gold" speech, and Eugene Victor Debs, the socialist who grasped the dangers of concentrated corporate capitalism for citizenship.

There's a wonderful story where Debs was giving a speech to a group of workers in Pennsylvania who were mostly Polish, and a journalist went up to one of them and found that this worker spoke no English, but he was crying with Debs's speech, and asked him—he must have spoken Polish or something—how come you're crying if you don't speak English? The answer was, "He spoke to us with his hands, and we understood." Debs, by the way, was eventually put into prison over World War I resistance, and while in prison still received six percent of the vote for presidency.

The electoral results provide a microcosmic view of the last 120 years of American history. In 1896, the entire center of the country voted for Bryan, while the coasts went for the Republican McKinley. The Bryan votes are the progressive ones; those for McKinley, the Republican or rightwing vote. When you get to 2012, the vote pattern has reversed itself: the center is now conservative and the coasts, liberal. It's a phenomenon worth thinking and talking about. What used to be the most progressive part of the country in the 1890s, now has become the least progressive part, and by 2016 it's even worse.

Debs, however, and the populists, for a variety of reasons, fail—the socialists failed in the end to become a viable political power, and never get more than about six to seven percent of the vote, though they do elect a sizeable number of local officials. Populism focuses too exclusively on the question of the coinage of silver and does not address the day-to-day problems of the working class. And why? What was the problem? Four matters come together here:

> One is the failure of populism and Debs to develop a successful political *cum* economic program.

The second—all of these need to be detailed, but you have to know that they're there—the rise and fall of the Industrial Workers of the World, the IWW, who have an extraordinarily good economic analysis, but fail, in fact explicitly refuse, to develop a political program that goes with it.

The third, and most important in some sense, is that the practice of politics changes. It is no longer an amateur sport, one might say, but becomes a professional sport. When Lincoln ran for the House in the 1850s, he said he would stay but one term—and did. This is not sortition, but it's a kind of mini-sortition. The idea was, "I'm going to go to Washington for a while, and then I'm going to come back and be with you fellow citizens at home, a regular person."

An aside here: I think in almost all the cases of sortition that have been presented at this conference, the speakers worried about making the results institutional but have failed to notice that there's a serious difference between those cases and the Greek situation in Athens. In Athens, there *was sortition: you were chosen by lot from different subsets to be a member of the boulé*, that is, of a permanently existing institution. So, the whole set of issues raised this morning about the problems of institutionalizing sortition was not a problem in Athens, where one was chosen by lot to an existing institution.

In any case, Lincoln stays only for one term. Until about 1910, the average tenure of a House of Representatives member is 1.5 terms. By the time you get to the mid-'20s, it's 10 years, five terms. Reelection rates are 84 percent. Being in politics is now a job, a profession, like being a doctor. Having a job, one needs to retain that job, one does not want to be fired. That means one has to get reelected, which is expensive, and we can follow that logic out: we see it today all the time. That's a major transformation in the way politics and citizenship works in the States, and it affects the whole question of sortition enormously and directly.

The fourth issue that matters is an important but little remembered paradigmatic incident in American politics—the 1919 Seattle general strike—during which, on their own, Seattle workers ran the city for five days—meals, hospitals, fire, feeding the children, delivering them milk, and so forth. The mainstream press called it a revolution and explicitly associated it with the new Bolshevik USSR Things eventually petered out, and what's important here is not only this action, which is the people rising up, but its failure, because what were the lessons that were drawn from that failure? It is precisely at this time—we're in 1919—that the Bolsheviks had apparently successfully consolidated the revolution. The model of the Russian Revolution is of signal importance thus to a wide group of Americans. *We* screwed up; *we* didn't succeed. How come those guys did it right? And eventually the Communist Party will provide a kind of direction for much on the Left, not always completely taken up, but a direction as to what one has to do in order to actually succeed. Ellen Schechter has written a fine book arguing that by the time you get to the 1930s, the Communist Party of the United States is the most progressive political movement in the country.

This leads us to a whole other set of issues, because we are in the 20th century, and the United States is moving into being part of a wider world in a much more extensive manner than it had before. Despite initial widespread opposition, America was drawn or pushed by Woodrow Wilson into the Great War; to an increasingly important degree the United States is involved with the rest of the world. And, as I said before, the Bolshevik Revolution had triumphed and, against all expectations, maintained power. In America, at this particular point—this is the end of the First World War and just after—economic, social, political pressures abound. By 1922, 20 percent of the workforce had gone out in 3,360 strikes.

How to deal with this labor unrest? How to deal with the attractions of socialism? Two lessons were drawn by many Americans from the failures of the end of the 19th century.

The first lesson is drawn by the progressives and their advocacy of a country in which social and economic problems are to be solved professionally by people with knowledge, by experts operating in the name of the public interest. We're already a good distance here from Bryan's 1896, "The people have a right to make their own mistakes."

Progressivism is an interesting phenomenon, relevant today: One of the things that is happening with the present pandemic, is that we are to a certain degree abdicating decisions to experts, which may be the right thing to do or not, but we are allowing them to make the decisions for us. Likewise, we see in the early 20th century the development of the discipline of "public administration"—nothing like it existed before. The first MBA program is established in 1908 and grows rapidly. And one gets this notion that somehow these problems will be solved not by the citizens, but by experts figuring out how to do it. This is the time of Taylorism; of Woodrow Wilson advocating a scientific approach to government—and that increasingly takes over.

Related to this is the development of the Social Gospel movement at the beginning of the 20th century. Progressive-minded Christians sought to make activity in this world the focus of reform activity. They are very concrete. They address specific problems: inequality, racism, slums, poor health conditions, child labor, and so forth. They argue that Christians are not to wait for the second coming of Christ to redeem the world, but to go out and change it. Jesus would not return, they held, until social justice had been achieved by us on this earth. William Jennings Bryan was closely affiliated with the movement, and it's worth noting that many of the most progressive elements in America around the turn of the 20th century were evangelical Christians. A very interesting question is what exactly has happened to them. See here the fine book by Tanya Luhrmann, *When God Talks Back,* which finds that evangelical Christians are more complicated than most of us think.

A second lesson—the first lesson is progressivism coupled with Social Gospel—is consequent to the success of the Bolshevik revolution. To a great degree, this shapes the progressive Left. If events like the 1919 Seattle strike went nowhere, progressives concluded, it must have been because those involved were, in the terms of a famous editorial of the strike, proceeding to go "we not where." What was needed was some idea of where or what one should proceed to, and the success of the Leninist Party was of great importance. Against all odds, the Bolsheviks not only took but maintained power. What did they know? And accordingly, the American Left, in the period 1921–45, must come to grips with the apparent success of the USSR For instance, in 1937 *The Nation* magazine publishes an editorial *during the purge trials* in Moscow saying that despite the trials the Soviet Union remained the best hope for mankind. We forget how and why it was possible to make such a claim.

An important element here as to how to deal with the success of the USSR in America can be traced to changes in the American Communist Party, the CPUSA, which, under the leadership of Earl Browder, seeks to fully Americanize itself and join a conflictual notion of social justice with being an American. In 1936, Browder runs for president on the slogan, "Communism is 20th- Century Americanism." The story here is extremely complicated, and to tell it one has to begin to intersect this part of the Left with various aspects of the New Deal, all of which focus upon the development of economic democracy as a prerequisite for vigorous citizenship. For there was much resistance. Particular to note here are two things: One is a strong domestic resistance to Left New Deal policies. In 1944, Vice-President Henry Wallace is denied being reappointed as vice president for the reelection of Roosevelt, and Truman is instead chosen. Truman is anti-Soviet and much more conservative, and has no global sense about the postwar and increasingly postcolonial world.

The second thing that happens is not domestic but international. The American Communist Party in 1940 dissolves and is replaced by the "Communist Political Association"—I cite from their founding document: "The Communist Political Association carries forth the traditions of Washington, Jefferson, Paine, Jackson, and Lincoln under the changing conditions of modern industrial society"—it sounds like socialism with American characteristics. The document continues: "It upholds the Declaration of Independence, the United States Constitution [these are Communists] and its Bill of Rights and the achievements of the American democracy against all the enemies of public liberties."[7] The Communist Left is essentially trying to turn itself into a leftwing pressure group in favor of economic democracy. And if you look at the sorts of things they support during the '30s and '40s, from Spain to civil rights to the arts and so forth, it is not a limited set of actions.

What happens, in 1945, is that the Soviets get very distressed at this, because, on the one hand, Yugoslavia is going its own way, as is, on the other hand and more importantly, China, where the revolution is about to succeed. Moscow is urging the Chinese Communists to stop their advance at the Yangtze River. The directive is ignored. I can tell stories about that at some length.

There is published in *Cahiers du communisme* a letter by a French Communist Party theorist named Jacques Duclos attacking the American Communist Party, or rather attacking Browder, and accusing him of American exceptionalism, ideological naivete, and about anything else one could fling at him. The letter had obviously been approved (and probably written) in Moscow. It could not be ignored. What Browder wanted was in fact to pursue and support the policies which had been agreed upon between the great powers in Tehran. The American Party leadership meets three times to consider the Duclos letter (I have the FBI transcripts from the bugging of the meeting), then expelled Browder and capitulated to Moscow. Two years later, the leadership was arrested and sentenced to jail terms and fines. The question after the Duclos letter is if one can still be on the progressive Left, perhaps a Communist, and fully an American citizen. That possibility fades, partly killed off by the Russians, but also by the knee-jerk reaction of the CPUSA leadership, and then of course with the Cold War.

The available political spectrum in the 1930s and the early '40s is much wider than that of 10 years later, and that is an enormously important fact. But it's for naught. East-West relations in '45–'46 focus particularly over the fate of Eastern Europe. The conceptualization that makes the construction of the Cold War possible derives from Kennan's long telegram about "containment," which allows policy planners to make sense of the confusions of Eastern Europe. That telegram becomes radicalized into a doctrine called NSC-68, which provides the basis for American foreign policy for the next 25 or 30 years.

In 1947, Congress is taken over by the Republicans, and a variety of domestic surveillance and loyalty testing programs—again a contraction of the political sphere—are put into place: they severely constrain citizen activity and the vision of an independent citizenship.

The Loyalty Board, McCarthyism, failure of Wallace's Progressive Party, the arrests and jailing of the leadership of the Communist Party, the loss of China, the apparent aggression that starts the Korean War, the fear of nuclear war after 1949—all these and more reinforce certain policies and attitudes and impede the possibility of the progressive notion of citizenship. A range of political paths that had been legitimately available to many up until the end of the Second World War are now thought un-American. A Congressional committee on "Un-American Affairs" investigates all that partook and partakes of that spectrum. Victor Navasky's *Naming Names* provides an excellent account of this as does E. J. Kahn's *The China Hands* of the purge of the State Department.

The 1950s find a rise in commercialism in the place of citizenship, and a certain homogenization of the country. My term for this homogenization is "a clam roll." Why? With the resources that became available post–World War II, people began to buy cars, and the Interstate Highway Program shortly came into being, which meant that one could drive 200–300 miles a day. Now if one lives and drives in and around Poughkeepsie, one knows where to go to eat. But if one has a car and has driven 300 miles, how does one know what is a good restaurant? And the genius of Howard Johnson was to build restaurants that served exactly the same thing all across the country. That's the clam roll. I loved the clam rolls. The clam roll was the same in Ohio, Illinois, and Indiana. You could depend upon it: the homogenization, as it were, of the country.

Thus, creeping conformism. Conformism tends to be resisted, but most often nonpolitically, e.g., the beatniks. The New Left begins to emerge from the early Civil Rights Movement and anti-anti-Communist movements among the students. By the way, as there has been talk at this conference about parallel *poleis*: the idea in the New Left is that the universities are parallel *poleis* because the students don't owe their job or anything to anyone.

The founding document of the Students for a Democratic Society, the Port Huron Statement, turns out to be not really about politics or citizenship; but about authenticity, of being yourself. There's very little on trade unions, or political parties, or anything like that. The document mentions not once, I believe, any of the things I've talked about here, or any of the resources that were available to it from American history. It is as if SDS thought it had to start things all over again. They do not even attempt to reinvent a wheel that already had been there; they think they need to start anew. There is eventually a glimmer of public participatory hope in some of the SDS programs, as well as in the Great Society, both of which, however, get undone by local interests or repression. With the later rise of social media (see here the work of Sherry Turkle), the disappearance of the public is increasingly prevalent. The project seems forgotten.

Now I am basically done, but let me tell you two things that could have happened. This, out of the 1944 State of the Union message, from Roosevelt: Americans are to have he says, "the right to useful and remunerative jobs; . . . to earn enough to provide adequate food. . . . ; the right of every farmer to raise and sell his products for a decent living; of every businessman to trade and buy without unfair competition; the right of every family to a decent home, to adequate medical care"—this is 1944!—"and the opportunity to achieve and enjoy good health; the right to adequate protection from the economic fears of old age, sickness, accident, and unemployment, and"—think again—"the right to a good education."[8] This is what Roosevelt wanted and would have pushed. But he died. Congress eventually gutted it.

A second thing that could have happened: Postwar in '45, the United Auto Workers (UAW) had foregone strikes during the war. As part of the Congress of Industrial Organizations (CIO) it entered negotiations with General Motors. The UAW automobile workers wanted everything to be subject to collective bargaining, not just wages and working conditions, but what products were made, how they were marketed, how they were priced. They wanted a full say about everything. They wanted what's called comanagement. They wanted to control their own life and the products of their own labor. Charlie Wilson, head of GM, said this is an idea from east of the Rhine and refused to even discuss the issues. The Taft-Hartley Act contains a clause that a union must certify that none of its leadership down to the shop level were Communist Party or fellow travelers, in order to be eligible to engage in collective bargaining. Approximately one-third of the leadership of the CIO fell into that category. The CIO caved. Progressive elements in the Labor Movement were eliminated. The CIO eventually joined the much more conservative American Federation of Labor, and that is the beginning of the death of unionism.

I started this talk with reference to Socrates. In the *Crito*, the next dialogue, Socrates, having been condemned to death, has been trying to explain to Crito why he doesn't really think he should flee, as Crito has urged him to do. And as he can't convince Crito by an argument, he tells a story. It's the story of a dream he says he had where the laws and commonality—*nomoi kai te koinon* in the Greek—come to speak to him as he awaits death and considers these urgings to flee. The laws point out to him that all that he—Socrates—is, is shaped by his being an *Athenian* citizen. He owes himself to Athens, which is not the same as those who voted to condemn him. He refuses to escape. And his understanding is this: *You learn what it is to be a citizen of your own polity from that polity even when or if others—how many others?—have forgotten or repressed or denied it. What needs revitalizing is the project.* And to do so may not be a trivial cost. Tellingly, the signers of the Declaration pledged their explicit willingness to die, as did the Puritans. As do figures like James Baldwin and Malcolm X.

America has always been a project, now less and less realized perhaps over time. What we need to do to revitalize democracy in this country is to learn from and practice elements of that project. One could do worse here than to cite the encomium from Pindar's Second Pythian Ode, a phrase which Nietzsche took as his touchstone. Excuse the Greek, but it's nice: *genoi hoios essi mathon*, which translates as "Having learned, become what you are."

There's a fuller story of this in my book, *Learning One's Native Tongue: Citizenship, Contestation, and Conflict in America* (Chicago UP), where I try to work this all out in some detail. I might say just in concluding, that today is the birthday of two people whose work has helped shape my talk here. One is Fredrich Nietzsche, and the other is Michel Foucault. I thank you.

Q&A with Allison Stanger

Allison Stanger: That was great. Well, you've given us a lot to chew on here, so it's quite a sweeping, wonderful, wonderful talk, and I thank you for it. And I have a whole series of questions about the history you're presenting, because I agree with you that America has always been a project for which citizens are willing to die, you know. And you traced the evolution of understandings of citizenship over time. And I think they've obviously very much changed. I might quibble with you over some bumps in the road there. So let me just throw some stuff out there and you can respond. And I'll say all this by prefacing it with I am married to a refugee from communist Czechoslovakia, so I spent—I have a degree in Soviet studies, so I spent in communist Soviet Union and in communist Czechoslovakia. So, I may have kind of a jaded view of communism, and let me just point out a couple of points:

First point: You said that in 1848 the term American was first used.

Tracy B. Strong: I misspoke, It was 1648.

AS: Okay, good, phew. So the crisis of—I guess your argument—It's a crisis of the project currently, the American project now, not a crisis of democracy. No?

TBS: Go ahead.

AS: I wanted to ask you to elaborate on that. But maybe we just bracket that so I can—I want to cluster some historical points and then come back to that. I like this idea of the original notion of citizens being virtuous coming from the Puritans. But that raises the really interesting question when you look at the history of exclusion of citizens in the United States, and you see women not getting the right to vote until the 20th century; yet culturally they're seen as the custodians of virtue. So how would you square that?

TBS: So the question is women aren't being heard, right? Women are virtuous, but it is private virtue. Their virtue is in fact to keep men behaving virtuously in public. Hence the prevalence of women, for instance, in the Temperance Movement, which is, don't let your men go out there and get smashed, he'll be a bad guy. But it's not a public sense of virtue. See here *The Feminization of American Culture* an old book by Ann Douglas. But that's the difference. There's a lot of complexity here. Women have the right to vote, for instance, in New Jersey up until 1804, so that changes back and forth. Alexander Keyssar has published a book called *The Right to Vote*. One of the things he shows in that book is that the United States is the only, should we call it, Western nation where the right to vote is more restricted at the end of the 19th century than it was at the beginning. It's quite stunning.

Now, the women are tricky because there are places where men and even some women are saying, oh, well they're citizens of course, but they don't have the right to vote, because having the right to vote requires this other set of criteria, this other quality, which women can't have. And there you get the sort of standard things: They should stay at home, they should raise children, it's all private, they are to be goody-two-shoes, they are to keep their men in line, but they aren't to be out there in the great wide world.

That changes. And the point I was making, though, the important point about the abolitionist and the feminist movement is that women lead those movements, and they therefore are in public, and that's the beginning really of a development which I think eventually results in the 1919 amendment making women citizen, giving women the right to vote, achieved, as I said, by a single vote majority in the Tennessee State House.

AS: This is sort of an interesting question you might comment on more generally, this notion of virtue being something that's in the public domain only?

TBS: No, there's public and private.

AS: Right. But is that distinction routinely made in political philosophy between a public realm and a private realm of virtue? I thought people were either virtuous or not virtuous. Am I wrong?

TBS: Yes. Having a public concern is a particular kind of virtue. If you are a woman, for a long time, if you are Black and so forth, you can't have public concerns because you're deemed incapable of it.

AS: Right, but what I guess I'm getting at, isn't that sort of a subtext rather than something that's stated explicitly?

TBS: Well, you can find it—It's in Rousseau, it's in Montesquieu,—there's a lot of political theory which does it. It's unfortunate, as one knows. But it's something to which there are counter-arguments, or counter-examples, more exactly, but they're normally phrased as examples. The closest one comes is the sort of aristocratic women probably in 18th-century France, where you begin to get something closer to it. In the States it just doesn't happen as far as I can tell.

AS: Except you have Tocqueville extolling American women in particular.

TBS: Yes, they're very good people.

AS: Just not good citizens.

TBS: No, they're citizens, but they can't vote. Tocqueville never said they should vote. This is the point I'm trying to make over all. Voting, for a long time, up till the Fourteenth Amendment, is seen as something which requires that you manifest certain kinds of qualities of being. Some people or groups are deemed—this is sexism—are deemed incapable of it—women, Blacks, and so forth. The argument in the South is we can't give Blacks the right to vote because they are children. We have to take care of them--Christian trusteeship, as Calhoun called it. The voting that is the participation in the public is separate from being a citizen, and what the Fourteenth Amendment does is it merges those two. That's how we still think of citizenship now, but it's a brand new idea in 1868, or it's an idea which, shall we say, is fully institutionalized in 1868.

AS: This is getting fascinating. I don't know if you're equally fascinated. We can take another line if you like, but isn't citizenship equated with voting in Athens?

TBS: Not for women. Not for slaves.

AS: But were they considered citizens? I don't think so.

TBS: Well, to be an Athenian citizen at that point you have to have an Athenian mother and an Athenian father. Therefore, women, Athenian mothers, can, are, in some sense Athenian, and in that sense, you could say they are in some sense citizens. I'd have to check precisely what language is used for that, so that's a good question.

AS: Okay. Let's—this is interesting—I want to push you a little bit, and then we'll turn it over to questions from the audience. I have a lot of questions, but just one or two more: You spoke of the attractions of socialism in the US and kind of presented it as an almost American feature. I would almost argue the exact opposite, that anti-communism—

TBS: Anti-socialism starts by the turn of the 20th century: it is linked with anarchism, syndicalism and so on in a very promiscuous manner. It is investigated by the Bureau of Investigation, the forerunner of the FBI—you can get microfilm of their reports. Anti-communism starts shortly after the Bolshevik Revolution as an accusation. As a full-blown national policy, it's not till after the Second World War.

AS: But Debs goes to prison for traitorous—

TBS: No, Debs goes to prison because he mentions something negative about the draft in one sentence of one speech in 1917. Until the United States declared war upon Germany in 1917, the popular opinion was overwhelmingly against going to war. And socialism—the argument you're making about socialism is a standard argument which has come down mainly from Europeans. Why is there no socialism in America? Well, there is an American kind of something called socialism, and if you look at the kinds of arguments which are made by the Knights of Labor or the Grange, or the Greenbackers, and so forth, they are in many ways one would say something akin to what we might call socialists. They don't call it that. Debs is the person who calls it that and declares himself a socialist after a particular set of developments. But it is socialism, shall we say, with American characteristics. There's a book by Alex Gourevitch, which pursues this; it's really very good.

But the difference that happens that I was trying to argue is that—one forgets the enormous impact that the success of the Bolshevik Revolution had upon the progressive elements of the American polity. An awful lot of Americans in the late '20s and '30s go to the USSR to find out and participate, women including—there's a big book on women going over to the Soviet Union to find out what's going on there. It has an enormous impact because the damn thing seems to work. Now whether or not it's actually working and what's going on is not the immediate issue.

You get complicated things as to who is going to oppose predatory capitalism? Well, it's not going to be the English, it's not going to be the French, and it's not going to be the Americans. The only world force that's doing it is—seems to be—the Soviets. At that point you're not worried really about the gulags—and I can talk more about the gulags—but you're not worried about those things; you're worried about the—These people say they're in favor of justice and social equality, and so forth. And it's a great strong example. I quoted from Frida Kirchwey, the editor of *The Nation* in 1937: she's saying the Soviet Union remains mankind's best hope—despite the purge trials. A stunning document.

AS: Well, you also have Debs making speeches where he's effectively traitorous, praising Russia as a superior model than the American model. And I guess my problem is this: How can you define something as American when it's actually being pedaled by a foreign power and all the movements are receiving money from Moscow?

TBS: This is the problem which the American party has to solve, and that's what Earl Browder is trying to do. The argument is that "Communism is 20th century Americanism"—and he got into a lot of trouble inside the Party. Partly because the Party was run in a Leninist manner he was able to impose himself, but he was strongly resisted, and when in fact the Duclos letter came out, the Party met three times. I actually have the documents of it because the Party's headquarters were bugged, and it was taken down by the FBI, so I have the FBI's bugging of the discussion, what to do about the Duclos letter. And he abolished the Party as a party, turned it into a political association, and so forth.

The terrible thing is that everybody in the Central Committee capitulates, including Elizabeth Gurley Flynn. I mean, they all toe Moscow's line, and it's a failure.

Now, what would have happened if Truman had not president? Would Moscow have responded differently? There were very worried about losing number-one status in the communist movement. They certainly don't mind losing Yugoslavia, they don't like it. They're very worried about China. There are long stories there I can go into. I interviewed the person who's the head of propaganda in Yen'an, a member of the Chinese Central Committee in '40s and '50s, Lu Ding Yi. And he told me with a sort of a slight smile in his eye, there was also anger though in his eye, "We did not get one bullet from the Russians. They didn't help us at all." I mean, he hated the Russians for their lack of support. The Russians tried, for instance, in '47-'48, to convince the Chinese Communists to stop their advance at the Yangtze River and leave the rest of the country to the Nationalists, and Mao said bullshit.

Other cute stories there: I was told in Yen'an that at the time that the Central Committee of the Chinese Party was making the important decisions, their radio link with Moscow would suddenly not work, so they could make the decision without consulting. But the Soviets are very worried about the Chinese, and if they lose China as subordinate and lose the United States as subordinate, they've lost the two major parties in the world. And therefore they've got to do something about it, and I think that's the source of the Duclos letter. We know that there were conflicts—and you would know this better because of your studies—but there were conflicts inside the leadership of the Soviet Union as to how to respond to the Tehran Declarations, and how to respond to the proposal of coexistence, and those kinds of things.

AS: Most definitely, yes. I have eight. Okay. We definitely want to turn it over to the audience. We're getting down into the weeds here. Please help up come back up out of the weeds. Questions. American citizenship. Roger.

Roger Berkowitz: Thanks, Tracy. It does strike me that you've told a story that might be called a Jeffersonian story without mentioning Jefferson.

TBS: I mentioned him once.

RB: You did mention—Okay. Where's Hamilton in this story?

TBS: Oh boy!

RB: And not just him, but like the urban story. I mean, this seems like a very agrarian American story, which has appeals on a lot of levels, but it seems to be focused on that. And maybe I'm wrong or missing something—

TBS: You want more? There's more. The one thing focused on, however, is that one of the things that happens over the course of time is that as conditions in the country change—expansion, things like that—the criteria that one has to meet to think of oneself as a citizen themselves change. And of them—and I did mention this—is that with the sudden growth, very rapid growth in the major cities of literate artisans, but who are non-propertied—something's got to be done with them. And in fact, Paine is the person who in fact argues for—this is now urban—for this possession of tools as a basis for citizenship. And his argument is strong enough, and the realities of the changing demographic situation are salient enough, that in fact Madison yields the property question at least in relation to the lower House. Now in 1820, I think it was, he does write another article where he says he really wishes we could have property qualifications for the upper house. This is when of course the Senate is not elected in the way that it is now, and he's hoping to retain some kind of notion of property on the grounds that I said. That's quite true.

But the Paine argument carries the day. And then you get this complex expansion which is not fundamentally urban, but becomes Free Soil, which goes on for a while. I mean, Chicago's a tiny little town until sometime after the Civil War. But there's a danger of a certain amount of agrarianism. Now Bryan and the Populists are often accused of being sort of agrarian goody-goodies. There are several books on the relation of populism to industrialization and the urban situation which are pretty convincing that that's a great deal of an exaggeration.

Now a lot of this has to do with the fact that American history is often written as if somehow your Jeffersonian model were the only thing or he only desirable thing. There's a certain amount of literature that came out, that started coming out in the '60s, saying that's not really the case. And then you get to books like David Montgomery's books on the working class and so forth in the early 20th century, and there's nothing of agrarianism there at that point. But we do retain a certain fondness for it—you know, when thinking of "being your own man," you tend to think of a farmer first and not of a person working in a factory.

AS: We've got a question right in the front row.

Audience Member: Hi. My takeaway from your talk, which I really appreciated, is just simply reminding us of the labor history of the United States, and whether we call it communist, or labor, or socialism, Kellogg's is on strike right now, nurses are on strike right now. The remaining elements of a union and labor movement in the US is active, and I guess the question you asked was who was going to take on predatory capitalism. And I think that that is a question that I wonder if citizens' assemblies can address. But who is going to take them on? Are they going to take them on? Are they going to have the power? Because I think it's obviously a question that has to be addressed, and I think it's one that we're—I know Kali talked about power and needing economic leverage. I think it's entered the space, but I feel like you've put the labor issue on the table.

TBS: The labor issue is absolutely on the table. By and large our sense of what makes labor successful are labor unions, and we know what's happened to labor unions, which are now very small except in certain parts of the public sector.

The number of strikes during the 1950s goes way down, and they're very quickly dealt with partly because there's legislation which allows them to be squashed and so forth.

There are interesting things being thought about. I have a colleague who's just written a very interesting article, on what he calls "Just Riots." Now, we're back to problems we had before today, which is, okay, you have a riot and so forth. What's the institutionalization? That doesn't happen. I have a graduate student who wrote about the demonstrations in Seattle over seven or eight years ago as an example of a new form of representation. But again you have the problem of nobody remembers those now. It's unclear, I don't know what it's like in Seattle. The general strike in Seattle lingered as a touchstone memory for some considerable period of time, and there's still a lot of people concerned with it there. It was actually an extraordinary event in American history.

But there's the question to which I don't know the answer, which is, what is the relationship between the kind of thing that you're talking about and the existence of social media? And I just don't know how that's going to work. And there are times when I'm relatively convinced that social media in fact, as Sherry Turkle wrote, makes us alone together. But there's also a way clearly in which social media can connect people to each other. I do know that in China the existence of cell phones has produced at certain times an interesting kind of local pressure upon the central power. It gets co-opted pretty easily, however. It's not coordinated here, or it's coordinated in various groups, most of which I'm not part of and we're not part of. I don't know to resolve that. But those are the issues that need to be thought through, and I think the social media questions is absolutely key. The last chapter of my book, which I have shamelessly posted, actually goes into the question of social media and what it does in terms of a sense of the public. Whatever kind of public it is, it's a different kind of public than the kind I'm talking about in the rest of the talk.

AS: We are unfortunately out of time. Please join me in thanking Professor Strong for a stimulating talk.

Notes

1. Langston Hughes, "Let America Be America Again," Academy of American Poets, poets.org/poem/let-america-be-america-again.
2. Frost, Robert, In the Clearing (New York: Holt, Rinehart and Winston, 1962).
3. Plato, Apology 17a, in Euthyphro, Apology, Crito, Phaedo, trans. Harold F. North (Cambridge, MA: Harvard University Press, 1966).
4. Abraham Lincoln, "The Perpetuation of Our Political Institutions," in The Collected Works of Abraham Lincoln, ed. Roy P. Blaser, 9 vols. (new Brunswick, NJ: Rutgers University Press, 1955) 1:113.
5. Cited in A. Keyssar, Right to Vote, 69; see the additional material in footnote 18, on his page 399. Frederick Douglas had said the same in 1861.
6. Robert Lowell, "For the Union Dead," Poetry Foundation, poetryfoundation.org/poems/57035/for-the-union-dead
7. See "Constitution of the Communist Political Association," in The Path to Peace, Progree and Prosperity: Proceedings of the Constitutional Convention of the Communist Political Association, New York, May 20-22, 1944 (New York: CPA, 1944), 47-51, marxists.org/history/usa/parties/cpusa/1944/05/0522-cpa-constitution.pdf
8. Franklin D. Roosevelt, "1944 State of the Union Address," January 11, 1944, TeachingAmericanHistory.org, https://teachingamericanhistory.org/document/state-of-the-union-address-3/

ESSAYS

Hannah Arendt, Storyteller

Matthew Longo

Hannah Arendt thought quite a lot about the power of stories.[1] This comes out clearly, for example, in her introduction to Walter Benjamin's *Illuminations* (1968), in which she lauds his penchant for collecting quotations as a means of uncovering shards of truth, wherever they may lie hidden. For Arendt, stories and storytelling were clearly not antithetical or inconsistent with argumentation, but rather seminally part of it. But in what ways might Hannah Arendt herself be considered a storyteller? And how might reading her in this way change the way we approach her arguments?

In what follows, I analyze an excerpt of Arendt's writing—the opening sequence of *Eichmann in Jerusalem*—in an attempt to show how it might be read as *descriptive storytelling*. Thereafter, I juxtapose it beside a more clear-cut example of storytelling in political theory, Nancy Hirschmann's discussion of obstructed abortion attempts by an unnamed mother in her 1996 article, "Toward a Feminist Theory of Freedom." By looking at these two examples in tandem I hope to show how, despite clear differences in style and framing, these authors use stories in similar ways—specifically toward what Ian Shapiro terms "problematizing redescription" (2005). In both cases, storytelling doesn't just aid their arguments rhetorically; rather it is part of their constitutive fabric.

A Tale of Two Stories

Hannah Arendt's Eichmann

In her classic, *Eichmann in Jerusalem*, Hannah Arendt details the Eichmann trial, which began on April 11, 1961, in the *Beth Hamispath*, or the House of Justice in Jerusalem. Like many stories (including Hirschmann's), Arendt's telling is culled not from the imagination or biblical yore but the world as it has unfolded in real (present) time. But Arendt's storytelling here is different than most, as what she is describing is based on her *own* experience in the courthouse; consequently, her account shares affinity with journalism, as well as with the ethnographic tradition of telling stories through fieldnotes.[2] Arendt's experience shapes how she portrays the events, and consequently the kinds of arguments this description engenders.

Although in some sense the whole book could be read as an extended instance of storytelling, for this essay I will home in on the descriptive scene-setting, which takes place at the very beginning. Here, she lays out the physical space of the trial, as well as the cast of characters who will take part in the proceedings. Arendt begins:

> "Beth Hamishpath"—the House of Justice: these words shouted by the court usher at the top of his voice make us jump to our feet as they announce the arrival of the three judges, who, bareheaded, in black robes, walk into the courtroom from a side entrance to take their seats on the highest tier of the raised platform. Their long table, soon to be covered with innumerable books and more than 1,500 documents, is flanked at each end by the court stenographers. Directly below the judges are the translators, whose services are needed for direct exchanges between the defendant or his counsel and the court. . . . One tier below the translators, facing each other and hence with their profiles turned to the audience, we see the glass booth of the accused and the witness box. Finally, on the bottom tier, with their backs to the audience, are the prosecutor with his staff of four assistant attorneys, and the counsel for the defense. . . .
>
> There is no doubt from the very beginning that it is Judge Landau who sets the tone, and that he is doing his best, his very best, to prevent this trial from becoming a show trial under the influence of the prosecutor's love of showmanship. Among the reasons he cannot always succeed is the simple fact that the proceedings happen on a stage before an audience, with the usher's marvelous shout at the beginning of each session producing the effect of the rising curtain. Whoever planned this auditorium in the newly built Beth Ha'am, the House of the People (now surrounded by high fences, guarded from roof to cellar by heavily armed police, and with a row of wooden barracks in the front courtyard in which all comers arc expertly frisked), had a theater in mind, complete with orchestra and gallery, with proscenium and stage, and with side doors for the actors' entrance. Clearly, this courtroom is not a bad place for the show trial David Ben-Gurion, Prime Minister of Israel, had in mind when he decided to have Eichmann kidnaped in Argentina and brought to the District Court of Jerusalem to stand trial for his role in the "final solution of the Jewish question." (Arendt 1963: 3; 4-5)

In this passage, Arendt uses description to depict the courthouse as spatially and aesthetically like the stage of a theater, imparting it as less a site for the impartial arbitration of truth than a forum for political hijinks. In her portrayal, the court is figuratively exposed for what she thinks it is: more a circus than a trial.

This description is not incidental to the argument—in many ways it *is* the argument. Without it, her critique would lack much of its evidentiary basis. For Arendt, the story provides a platform for interpretation; she is inviting you to see the world as she saw it. The story, then, is not simply an illustration of a claim, but rather the grounds on which it may be contested; how it might be falsified, or subject to redescription and reinterpretation. Arendt continues from the previous quotations by framing the problem: the gap between what justice demands (based on the actions of Adolf Eichmann), and the broader moral and political agenda of the state of Israel (justice for the inhumane treatment of the Jews). It is not random but rather essential to the point of her storytelling that it is in this context that we get the first description of Eichmann in all of his unpersonable personality:

> Justice demands that the accused be prosecuted, defended, and judged, and that all the other questions of seemingly greater import – of "How could it happen?" and "Why did it happen?," of "Why the Jews?" . . . be left in abeyance. Justice insists on the importance of Adolf Eichmann, son of Karl Adolf Eichmann, the man in the glass booth built for his protection: medium-sized, slender, middle-aged, with receding hair, ill-fitting teeth, and nearsighted eyes, who throughout the trial keeps craning his scraggy neck toward the bench (not once does he face the audience), and who desperately and for the most part successfully maintains his self-control despite the nervous tic to which his mouth must have become subject long before this trial started. On trial are his deeds, not the sufferings of the Jews, not the German people or mankind, not even anti-Semitism and racism. (Arendt 1963: 5)

Arendt's objective in this use of narrative description is not merely to point out the shortcoming of the court, but rather, by placing the court in context, to make sense of its actions. It is by seeing how the court is situated, how the prosecutors and judges behaved, that we can make sense of some of its incongruous features—the trial's "irregularities and abnormalities" (Arendt 1963: 253), such as the decision not to make ethnic distinctions (between Jews and nonJews),[3] and to insist the court could only be Jewish. Outside of the context in which the court was situated, such decisions are difficult to explain. But once we are transported—by storytelling—into the courtroom-cum-theater, we begin to understand. Here we see how the methodological intervention—descriptive storytelling—drifts into and furnishes the substance of her argument.

Arendt uses descriptive storytelling throughout the book as a way to anchor her argument about the way in which the trial was compromised, and to articulate the difficulty of linking abstract moral conceptions (about evil, for example, or humanity) into the particularist language of law. Indeed, it is precisely because of its circus-like setting that no one in the Israeli courthouse—neither on the stage nor in the crowd—could appreciate what she took to be the central puzzle of the trial: the fact that however despicable he was on paper, Eichmann in body wasn't a monster. This was obvious to Arendt, who sat through the trial as an observer not a participant, and was thus able to witness Eichmann for who he really was. In her writing, Arendt *must* convey this point through description because the real sense of him was "never reported."[4]

Arendt's depiction of the Eichmann trial, and specifically its dramatic staging is clearly an example of description. But is it also storytelling? To answer this question, it is helpful to turn to a more clear-cut case of storytelling within political theory, to see whether they might be pursuant to similar ends.

Nancy Hirschmann's Unnamed Mother

In her article, "Toward a Feminist Theory of Freedom," published in *Political Theory* in 1996, Nancy Hirschmann begins with Isaiah Berlin's classic division of negative and positive liberty, and uses this as a prompt to reassess the debate on feminist freedom. But first she begins with a story that helps frame the problem:

> The March 15, 1992, issue of the *New York Times* ran an article about a twenty-three-year-old unemployed single mother in West Virginia who became pregnant as a result of date rape. Due to federal policy, she had trouble locating an abortion clinic, but finally found one four hours away in Charleston. They told her she was seventeen weeks pregnant and they performed abortions only until sixteen weeks, and so they referred her to a clinic in Cincinnati, Ohio, that would perform an abortion up to nineteen and a half weeks for a cost of $850. When she went there a week and half later, however, she was told she was actually twenty-one weeks pregnant, and so the second clinic referred her to a clinic in Dayton, Ohio, that would perform the abortion for $1,675. She refinanced her car, sold her VCR, borrowed money, and went to Dayton. That clinic said that she was a high-risk patient because of an earlier Caesarean delivery, that she would have to go to Wichita, Kansas, and that it would cost $2,500. At this point, she decided that she no longer could manage the cost and logistics. Being opposed to adoption, she decided to have the baby and to try and love it the same way that she loves her other child. (Hirschmann 1996: 46)

She follows this excerpt with a devastating question: "*Can we say that this woman has freely chosen her role as mother?*" Hirschmann argues that western political philosophy offers us no way of answering this. The story is not revisited, except in passing, and thus its role is limited to this powerful provocation. Moreover, it is not itself descriptive—certainly not in the manner of Arendt's treatment of the Eichmann trial. So, what can we say is the significance of this instance of storytelling?

A couple of points jump out. First, the point of this example is not to suss out our priors or provide evidence for an argument, but rather to do the opposite: to articulate questions that lie beyond our reach. In this sense, the story is told with the intention of presenting the world in deeper complexity than we commonly do in political theory and thus provide a warrant for (re) classification. In this case, the story is used to cast doubt upon classic ways we go about thinking about freedom, not just Berlin's negative/positive divide, but also the distinction between internal and external constraints on action, as well as similarly simplistic dichotomies, such as formal/effective freedom and so forth.

But the story doesn't merely lend complexity to our field of view. It also furnishes the grounds for the argument itself, which will draw from that complexity unto a theory of contextuality—that to understand what makes freedom meaningful we must first appreciate how people (in this case women) evaluate the relative significance of the barriers they face and the competing values against which their freedom claims are situated. This sets up the argument she wants to outline, which is that for women to achieve freedom, they must first reclaim the discourse of what is valuable, which covers over the sexism at the heart of "choice" (and thus liberalism) due to the constructed nature of society. To do this, it is imperative to foreground women's experiences:

> The task for feminist theorists is to stake out an overtly political territory of values ... that would allow theorists to point out the ways in which patriarchal practices and customs deny women access to the resources they need to satisfy these values. In this, *women's experiences* provide a powerful basis for highlighting the frequent sexism of liberal theory, precisely because these experiences often lie at the crossroads of Enlightenment ideology of agency and choice with modern practices of sexism. (Hirschmann 1996: 48; italics mine)

In other words: we cannot separate freedom from the terms by which it is encountered—a point performatively embodied by her story, and the detailing of women's experiences, and which she, by argument, seeks to tease out. Returning to Berlin, her point is that once we take seriously the contextual and constructed nature of the world, the clean internal/external division Berlin establishes falls apart, as does the pretense of universalist models of citizenship (pace Iris Marion Young):

> [We must start] by challenging the naturalist basis to freedom altogether. . . . The desires and preferences we have, our beliefs

> and values, our way of defining the world are all shaped by the particular constellation of personal and institutional social relationships that constitute our individual and collective histories. Even the most intimate and supposedly 'internal' aspects of our being, such as our sexuality, must be understood in terms of the historical relations and actions that have imported meaning to our bodies. Context is what makes meaning possible, and meaning makes 'reality.' (Hirschmann 1996: 51-2)

According to Hirschmann, patriarchal values determine how we define freedom, and why we consider it to be meaningful. This challenges both dimensions of the internal/external divide. Returning to Berlin, this forces us to radically expand what negative liberty entails, because the types of external boundaries women face are also constitutive of who they are. It would also make us doubt positive liberty, as the things we consider to be "internal barriers" are externally generated. Hirschmann's argument is thus a critique of liberalism more broadly, and its inability to account for gender domination. To break this patriarchal mode, we need to begin with the contingencies of our evaluations of freedom, borne of experience – hence the importance of stories, which furnish both the frame for her argument, as well as the basis of its substantiation.

Storytelling and Redescription

With this juxtaposition in mind, we can now revisit the questions posed at the outset. What would it mean to view Hannah Arendt as a storyteller? And how does this implicate how we read her arguments? In what follows, I argue that storytelling allows both authors—Arendt and Hirschmann —to engage in what Ian Shapiro calls "problematizing redescription." Despite massive differences in the kinds of stories they tell and the ways in which they tell them, in both cases storytelling destabilizes existing narratives, thereby helping adumbrate knotty moral problems.

This comes through clearly in Arendt's description of the Eichmann trial in which she takes a problem we all intuitively understand—the Nazi persecution of Jews—and uses descriptive storytelling to crack open this reductive veneer, taking us out of the shallow rendering of what the trial was about and instead show us what was *actually* happening. By describing the setting and the actors, and analyzing the way statements were transmitted and received, she portrays a complicated dynamic within the trial; rather than show how law and justice work side by side—as was the trial's intention—she reveals the opposite, how they might be parasitic upon one another. The same goes for her description of Eichmann, far from the simple rendering of him as a cog in the Nazi killing machine, she portrays him in all his complexity, and in doing so creates a portrait that resists binary categorization. In both cases, she took something we thought was clear, and through the use of storytelling, muddies it up.

In the case of Hirschmann's unnamed mother, storytelling serves a similar purpose: its aim is to clarify a problem, not substantiate an answer. In this case, what the muddying detail of the story exposed was precisely the inability of the western tradition to appreciate the constraints on this woman's plight. Here the messiness of the story was precisely its purchase; the problem would not have been apparent had all the complexifying detail been filtered away. Rather than reduce moral problems down to their essential rudiments, Hirschmann shows us (through the act of storytelling) that this is precisely what obscures the moral problem in the first place, thereby leaving us incapable of solving it.

For both Arendt and Hirschmann, it is clear that storytelling was essential to the argument; and the stories told served similar roles, despite their difference in form. As both authors recognized, it is precisely by digging into the world in all of its messiness that we can see arguments we might have missed, or reconsider assumptions taken for granted, thereby furnishing the ground whereby those understandings might be revised or replaced.

Conclusion

Such a short treatment of Arendt-as-storyteller is of course unsatisfying and provisional. The depiction of the trial and courthouse in *Eichmann in Jerusalem* is just one example in her vast corpus. The point here was not to be exhaustive or to suggest that all her writing can and should be read in this way (or that there would be no cost to doing so). Rather it was to suggest that storytelling may play a broader role in her argument than we usually consider. By juxtaposing her writing beside Hirschmann's, we can see clearly how this might be true and what role it might play —specifically as a form of problematizing redescription. By analyzing Arendt in this way, my hope is to reveal the incredible powers of storytelling she engages in *Eichmann* and encourage readers to view this kind of descriptive prose as existing in the service of her argument, rather than as something altogether discrete.

Work Cited

Arendt, Hannah, 1963, *Eichmann in Jerusalem: A Report on the Banality of Evil* (New York: Penguin Books).

Arendt, Hannah, 1968, "Introduction: Walter Benjamin: 1892-1940," in *Illuminations* (New York: Harcourt, Brace & Jovanovich), pp. 7-58.

Benhabib, Seyla, 2000, *The Reluctant Modernism of Hannah Arendt* (Maryland: Rowman & Littlefield).

Hirschmann, Nancy, 1996, "Toward a Feminist Theory of Freedom," *Political Theory*, p. 42:1, pp. 46-67.

Longo, Matthew and Bernardo Zacka, 2019, "Political Theory in an Ethnographic Key," *American Political Science Review*, p. 113:4, pp. 1066-1070.
Shapiro, Ian, 2005, *The Flight from Reality in the Human Sciences* (Princeton: Princeton University Press).
Young, Iris Marion, 1990, *Justice and the Politics of Difference* (Princeton: Princeton University Press).
Zacka, Bernardo, Brooke Ackerly, Jakob Elster, Signy Gutnick Allen, Humeira Iqtidar, Matthew Longo and Paul Sagar, 2021, "Political Theory with an Ethnographic Sensibility," *Contemporary Political Theory*, p. 20:2, pp. 385-418.

Notes

1. For a scholarly discussion of this subject, see Benhabib 2000: 91.
2. For more on how ethnographic methods fit into political theory, see: Longo & Zacka 2019; Zacka et al 2020.
3. Indeed, the prosecutor, Hausner, went so far as to remark that if they decide to "charge [Eichmann] also with crimes against nonJews," it is not because he committed those crimes, but instead simply "because we make no ethnic distinctions" (Arendt 1963: 6). By Arendt's reading, this distilled simply to the point that they cared little for what crimes Eichmann had committed, but rather instead about what crimes the Jews had suffered.
4. She makes this point here: "Despite all the efforts of the prosecution, everybody could see that this man was not a 'monster,' but it was difficult indeed not to suspect that he was a clown. And since this suspicion would have been fatal to the whole enterprise . . . his worst clowneries were hardly noticed and almost never reported" (Arendt 1963: 54).

REVIEWS

Amor Spectatoris: On Samantha Rose Hill's Love of the Spectator

Hannah Arendt by Samantha Rose Hill
Reaktion Books, 2021

Review by Shaan Sachdev

There is, among some of our best young cultural critics, a certain distaste for the earnest eulogizing of intellectuals past. This temperance serves partly to atone for historical words and deeds that do not measure up to contemporary ethical standards. It also defers to a vogue impression that the very aesthetic of excitement is somehow . . . passé. A tone of glamorously phlegmatic irony is preferred. One sees it in new nonacademic writing about Hannah Arendt, whether it's Maggie Nelson pointing to Arendt's "sneering" idea of freedom[1], or Rebecca Panovka on Arendt's "snide, melodramatic, dis[dain] of the concept of factual verification,"[2] or Jackson Arn on how Arendt's Eichmann theory "struts on, swatting facts out of its way."[3]

There's something admirable about such rhetorical poise. It is grounded in moral certainty—one might even call it omniscience—about which side of the culture war is ultimately correct. It sneers at sneerers. It shames political ambivalence. It casts off naivete at all costs. But among these costs are humor, joy, surprise, and the unembarrassed *wonder* that feeds off neither moralizing nor activism but the public act of thinking earnestly, vividly, deftly, intrepidly.

When Samantha Rose Hill wrote the final pages of *Hannah Arendt*, at a café in New York City, she openly wept. A man nearby asked her what was wrong. "I told him I had to kill my best friend," Hill said in an interview with *Guernica* last fall. "I fell in love with Arendt 20 years ago. It's been a long romance, but writing this biography, I had to finally let go."[4]

In 1969, at Karl Jaspers's funeral, Arendt, wearing a black dress and ringing with grief, said about her own mentor, her lifelong paternal guide:

> We do not know, when a man dies, what has come to pass. We know only: he has left us. We depend upon his works, but we know that the works do not need us. . . . But the simple fact that these books were once a lived life, this fact does not go directly into the world or remain safe from forgetfulness. That about a man which is most impermanent and also perhaps most great, his spoken word and his unique comportment, that dies with him and thus needs us; needs us who think of him. Such thinking

> brings us to a relationship with the dead one, out of which, then, conversation about him springs and sounds again in the world.[5]

For all her talk about writing in order to understand, not influence, as she averred to Günter Gaus in 1964, Arendt, at this point in her life, had to have known she'd already been touched, *caressed*, by Fama, the Roman goddess of fame.[6] She'd have known that streams and swells of readers, after her disappearance, would've remembered her, thought of her, spoken with her, and thus brought her work and thinking to life—to immortality, "at home in the world of everlastingness," as she once described it.[7]

"Posthumous fame is usually preceded by the highest recognition among one's peers," she wrote in the introduction to the first collection of Walter Benjamin's translated works.[8] Arendt was not only the lustrous sylph at the center of the New York intellectuals. She was also at the center of public debates and institutions. She taught at Columbia, the University of Chicago, Princeton, and the New School. She was on the boards of the *American Scholar* and National Translation Center. She was the Committee on Social Thought's delegate to the White House. And this is just a cross section of her dense and dynamic resume, which Hill steadily develops in *Hannah Arendt*, our newest biography of Arendt in the lineage of immortalizations that started with Elizabeth Young-Bruehl's 1982 epic, *For Love of the World*.

This is not to say that Arendt was vainglorious. She wrote sheepishly to Jaspers that she'd been reduced to a "cover girl" when she saw herself on the front page of the *Saturday Review of Literature* in 1951.[9] She believed her principled protection of her private life correspondingly preserved her space to think. She avoided interviews in English and confessional writing. It's easy to forget that it wasn't until Young-Bruehl's biography that Arendt's relationship with Martin Heidegger came to the public's hungry attention. And yet, as she was writing her final work, *The Life of the Mind*, Arendt couldn't help but profess to her dear friend Mary McCarthy that it was to be her "crowning achievement." There's a difference, after all, between the glossy egocentrism of the celebrity face and the less persona-driven glory of illumination. Arendt wrote to understand and she wrote in public because she was talented enough at understanding to share it, to fill in gaps, to teach.

Books about Arendt's life and ideas have showered so heavily upon the Western textosphere in the last half century that the historian Walter Laqueur wrote an essay in 1998 titled "The Arendt Cult." Today, her most beautiful, literary, sparkling biography remains *For Love of the World*. Hill calls it a "momentous feat" and a quick flip through *Hannah Arendt*'s index reveals the enduring indispensability of Young-Bruehl's research.

So why read *Hannah Arendt*, the latest in the "Critical Lives" series, published by Reaktion Books in August 2021? For one thing, Samantha Rose Hill, professor at the Brooklyn Institute for Social Research and Senior Fellow at the

Hannah Arendt Center, is part of the cult. This doesn't mean she's breathless or toadying. But it does mean she's transparently and unironically animated by Arendt's ideas. It means she regularly posts Arendt's photographs and syllabi and favorite cocktails on Twitter, and that she weeps at coffee shops while typing through Arendt's sudden, fatal heart attack in 1975. It means she spent many months trawling the Hannah Arendt Archive at the Library of Congress in Washington, D.C., the German Literature Archive in Marbach, the Hannah Arendt Library at Bard College, and the Manuscript Reading Room at the New York Public Library. It means, just as Arendt memorized the words of her beloveds, among them Kant, Homer, and Benjamin, and just as Arendt referred to Rahel Varnhagen, a Jewish intellectual socialite who died 70 years before she was born, as her "closest friend," that Hill also has a lively and loving relationship with the words and unique comportment of a woman who died before *she* was born. As a consequence of this passionate devotion, Hill was able to incorporate fresh letters, poems, and details into her book. She was also able, as she said in another interview, to construct the fullest accounts thus far of Arendt's exile from Germany, her internment in Gurs, France, and her escape to the United States from Nazi-occupied France.[10]

But there's a more important reason *Hannah Arendt* is worth reading. Our age, like all ages, swirls with distinctions. If the cult has a principal mythos, it centers upon Arendt's resounding capacity to contextualize and distinguish—to situate a thing or event in history and then decide what it is, what it isn't, and what this means. Of course, she wasn't a perfect thinker. She erred. She misjudged. She abandoned empathy. The model of a perfect thinker today seems to be one who has never expressed an offensive thought. Yet, "there are no dangerous thoughts," as the famous Arendtian maxim goes—"thinking itself is dangerous." And so surely there are no perfect thinkers either. Thinking—the soundless inner-dialogue between one and oneself— inquires, strays, unsettles, offends, gnaws upon premises, unthreads ideologies, and, all the same, like moonlight in a black forest, it dazzles.

The point is that Arendt was as good a thinker as they come. She shows us *how* to think. She was a "grand and incessant theorist," the literary critic Alfred Kazin recalled.[11] "What struck one at first meeting Hannah Arendt," said her old friend Hans Morgenthau, according to the writer Barry Gewen, "[was] the vitality of her mind, quick—sometimes too quick—sparkling, seeking, and finding hidden meanings and connections beneath the surface of man and things."[12]

Unsurprisingly, it's the eidetic gusto of Mary McCarthy's obituary that most dramatically capsulizes Arendt's gift:

> . . . thought, for her, was a kind of husbandry, a humanizing of the wilderness of experience—building houses, running paths and roads through, damming streams, planting windbreaks. The task

> that had fallen to her, as an exceptionally gifted intellect and a representative of the generations she had lived among, was to apply thought systematically to each and every characteristic experience of her time—anomie, terror, advanced warfare, concentration camps, Auschwitz, inflation, revolution, school integration, the Pentagon Papers, space, Watergate, Pope John, violence, civil disobedience—and, having finally achieved this, to direct thought inward, upon itself, and its own characteristic processes.[13]

As Hill takes us through each of Arendt's major works, summarizing its essential ideas with the crisp economy for which the "Critical Lives" series is reputed, she warns us against relying too heavily upon Arendt's distinctions and categories. Arendt was, it's true, wary of historicism. She'd taken to heart Walter Benjamin's essay, "Theses on the Philosophy of History," which he opens by quoting the German philosopher Hermann Lotze: "One of the most remarkable characteristics of human nature is, alongside so much selfishness in specific instances, the freedom from envy which the present displays toward the future." And while Arendt's writing is marked by propulsive, sometimes even plangent, historical assertions, she manifestly held *rethinking* in high esteem. She'd alter ideas. She'd reformulate propositions. She'd redistribute loyalties. (Perhaps this is another way of saying that the persistent and energetic will to understand more aptly demonstrates a thinker's capacities than the thoughts themselves, which float around the cosmos, awaiting capture by anyone.)

Still, a dilemma arises when someone who is prolifically knowledgeable holds historicism at bay. Hill insisted, in her interview with *Guernica*, that "Arendt would have been very wary of her work being used as an analogy to understand our present political conditions." Yet, Hill herself cannot help it. Our age's pressing political and social questions speckle, punctuate, and guide her interpretations of Arendt's books and essays. And why not? Arendt did the same thing, in some way, every time she placed a notion in its lineage or found a hidden connection beneath a surface.

This brings us back to the more important reason *Hannah Arendt* is worth reading. Among the downsides of the distinctly modern universalization of literacy is not only the sheer volume of rhetoric with which one must contend, but also the dilutions, simplifications, and obfuscations of meaning that predictably have followed. If Arendt's overriding contention was "with the present state of the historical and political sciences and their growing incapacity for making distinctions," as Hill tells us, citing a letter Arendt wrote to the political scientist Eric Voegelin, then perhaps we can draw both on her spirit for theorizing as well as a few of her theories to salvage some of our most deflated language and look upon our world with clearer minds.

Many of Arendt's distinctions remain highly useful. Take her insights about power structures. In an age where the highest levels of media and politics employ the careless phraseologies of our lowest common denominators, our observations of reality hanker for some keenness. Arendt's definition of totalitarianism, for example, was much more precise than its various alarmist renditions during the last presidential administration—she argued that it was distinct, Hill writes, "from authoritarianism, tyranny and fascism, and rested on the radical atomization of the individual, elimination of spontaneity and political freedom. Its defining element was the instrumentalization of terror and construction of concentration camps."

Or, take the stratification of human life that Arendt presented in *The Human Condition*. When poet W. H. Auden reviewed the book in 1959, Hill writes, he suggested "it be read almost like a dictionary of conceptual definitions: earth, labor, work, action, private, social, public, political, promises, forgiveness." As the technologically expedited socialization of our own thought and action reaches a zenith that Arendt might never have imagined, her distinctions between the public, private, and social realms can aid us, however eerily, in grasping for *some* ideal of political freedom in the 21st century.

And of course, Arendt's defense of the right to social prejudice, not to mention her firm distinctions between opinion and ideology (and thus between prejudice and racism), can function like flash grenades in our oft intolerably intolerant conversations about identity politics. It is amid these matters that Hill most perceptibly hints at Arendt's surmisable disapproval. In her summary of Arendt's famously incendiary essay, *Reflections on Little Rock*, Hill writes: "Politics organized around identity cannot sustain or confer political freedom, because it tries to create a universal subject." And as far as revolutions go, she reminds us that Arendt didn't think they were simply a question of "putting a different set of people at the head of the government or of permitting some segment of the population to rise into the public realm." One can only wonder if Arendt, who weathered the Gestapo, an internment camp, and a near-fatal car accident, would have survived affronted students and the ensuing academic and publishing fallouts had she written frankly about the political prominence of identity in the 2020s.

In a 1963 essay, Elizabeth Hardwick considered the life of the writer in New York: "A certain pleasure, or relief, lies in the assurance that a genuine paranoid solidity cannot be absorbed by American life, that it will not break to the crush of the tooth. And that is a sort of role, perhaps."[14]

Arendt might have said this was the role of the *spectator*—she who chooses to step back from the stage to watch the actors who submit to the festival of life. "Only the spectator occupies a position that enables him to see the whole play," she once wrote, "as the philosopher is able to see the kosmos as a harmonious ordered whole."[15]

The spectator, withdrawing from habit, orthodoxy, and bureaucracy, is neither inactive nor indifferent, neither supercilious nor unexcited. Quite the contrary: her exuberance for life, for understanding the world, for delivering judgments, make us want to turn to her, think of her, converse with her, hold her among our dearest friends.

Notes

1. Nelson, Maggie, 2022, *On Freedom: Four Songs of Care and Constraint* (Toronto: McClelland & Stewart).
2. Panovka, Rebecca, "Men in Dark Times: How Hannah Arendt's Fans Misread the Post-Truth Presidency," *Harper's Magazine*, July 14, 2021, harpers.org/archive/2021/08/men-in-dark-times-hannah-arendt-post-truth/.
3. Jackson Arn, "Thinking the Worst of Ourselves," *The Hedgehog Review*, hedgehogreview.com/issues/who-do-we-think-we-are/articles/thinking-the-worst-of-ourselves, fall 2021.
4. Penaluna, Regan, and Samantha Rose Hill, "Samantha Rose Hill on Hannah Arendt: 'You See the Politics on Her Face,'" *Guernica*, October 25, 2021, guernicamag.com/samantha-rose-hill-on-hannah-arendt-you-see-the-politics-on-her-face/.
5. Samantha Rose Hill, 2021, *Hannah Arendt* (London: Reaktion Books, p. 182).
6. "Hannah Arendt 'Zur Person' Full Interview (with English Subtitles)," 2013, YouTube Video, *YouTube*, youtube.com/watch?v=dsoImQfVsO4.
7. Arendt, Hannah, 1977, *Between Past and Future: Eight Exercises in Political Thought* (New York: Penguin).
8. Benjamin, Walter, 1978, *Illuminations: Walter Benjamin* (New York: Schocken).
9. Young-Bruehl, Elisabeth, 2004, *Hannah Arendt: For Love of the World* (New Haven Conn.; London: Yale University Press).
10. "Samantha Rose Hill Talks with the Maroon about Her New Biography, Hannah Arendt," *The Chicago Maroon,* 2022, chicagomaroon.com/article/2022/5/16/samantha-rose-hill-talks-maroon-new-biography-hannah-arendt/.
11. Kazin, Alfred, n.d. "Woman in Dark Times," *The New York Review of Books*, 1982, nybooks.com/articles/1982/06/24/woman-in-dark-times/.
12. Gewen, Barry, "Hans Morgenthau and Hannah Arendt: An Intellectual Passion," *The National Interest*, August 25, 2015. nationalinterest.org/feature/hans-morgenthau-hannah-arendt-intellectual-passion-13682.
13. McCarthy, Mary, "Saying Good-by to Hannah," *The New York Review of Books*, 1976, nybooks.com/articles/1976/01/22/saying-good-by-to-hannah/.
14. Hardwick, Elizabeth, "Grub Street: New York," *The New York Review of Books*, 1963, nybooks.com/articles/1963/02/01/grub-street-new-york/.
15. Arendt, Hannah, 1981, *The Life of the Mind: The Groundbreaking Investigation on How We Think* (San Diego, Calif., Harcourt Brace Jovanovich).

370 Riverside Drive, 730 Riverside Drive: Hannah Arendt und Ralph Ellison

by Marie Luise Knott
Matthes & Seitz Berlin, 2022

Review by Roger Berkowitz

On May 23, 1941, Hannah Arendt arrived in New York City with her husband Heinrich Blücher. Her journey began after she was arrested in Berlin in 1933 for her work with the German Zionists. She charmed the young policeman who was interrogating her, and he let her go. She fled to Paris. Once the war broke out, she was interned in a concentration camp in Gurs, France. She escaped and found Blücher in Marseille. She and Blücher were stateless, but they secured travel papers from the Varian Fry network. When she arrived in New York, she telegraphed her ex-husband Günther Anders who was living in California, "We're saved."

In New York, Arendt and Blücher received a stipend from the Zionist Organization of America and found a room in what was then a tenement building for immigrants at 317 West 95th Street. Eight years later they moved to 130 Morningside Drive, just north of Columbia University, and then, later, Arendt and Blücher found the apartment they would live in until their death, at 370 Riverside Drive on the corner of 109th Street.

Arendt's apartment at 370 Riverside Drive was only 41 blocks south of Ralph Ellison's apartment on 730 Riverside. That palindromic accident is the source of the title of Marie Luise Knott's book *370 Riverside Drive, 730 Riverside Drive: Hannah Arendt und Ralph Ellison*.

Knott's inquiry into Arendt and Ellison takes as her point of departure a short letter Arendt wrote to Ellison dated July 29, 1965. The letter is a response to an interview Ellison gave to Robert Penn Warren that was published in the latter's book *Who Speaks for the Negro?* In that interview, Ellison had offered a critique of Arendt's essay "Reflections on Little Rock," written in 1957 and only published in 1959. The interview carries the title "Naked Violence and the Ideal of Sacrifice," and is reprinted in German translation in Knott's book.

Arendt's "Reflections on Little Rock" is probably her most notorious piece of writing; that is saying a lot given that she is also the author of *Eichmann in Jerusalem*, her account of the trial of Adolf Eichmann that unleashed one of the largest scandals in intellectual letters of the 20th century. The only reason Arendt's critique of the decision to forcibly integrate public schools in the American South was not as controversial as her book on Eichmann is that while the latter had many supporters and became *the* classic account of the Eichmann trial, the former was universally panned and largely ignored. For more than 60 years, Arendt's essay on Little Rock has been largely ignored, seen as an embarrassment for Arendt's defenders as well as her critics.

Something in Ellison's interview clearly moved Arendt. She dictated a brief letter that begins "Dear Mr. Ellison." Arendt concedes immediately: "You are entirely right: it is precisely this 'ideal of sacrifice' which I didn't understand; and since my starting point was a consideration of Negro kids in forcibly integrated schools, this failure to understand caused me indeed to go into an entirely wrong direction." Arendt adds that all the criticisms she received from her "liberal" friends had not bothered her. And yet, she continues, "I knew that was somehow wrong and thought I hadn't grasped the element of stark violence, of elementary bodily fear in the situation. But your remarks seem to me so entirely right, that I now see that I simply didn't understand the complexities of the situation."[1] As Knott observes wryly, the letter contains "Twenty short lines about a burning political question." (11)

Arendt's letter is not to be found in Ellison's papers. We don't know if Ellison read the letter; if he received the letter; or even if Arendt ever sent it. It exists only as a carbon copy in Arendt's papers in the Library of Congress, on which the name "Ellison" is underlined in pencil.

Letters are missives that seek an answer or at least ask to be read. "Essays," Knott writes, "are excursions." Her short book is such an excursion, an inquiry into a series of interlocking riddles: Did Arendt send the letter? Did Ellison read it? What can the intersection of Arendt and Ellison teach us about race, democracy, and the United States? And, why did Arendt write the letter?

Something in Ellison's interview spoke to Arendt, Knott tells us. But what so impressed itself on Arendt that, eight years after writing her essay and after numerous often scathing criticisms that left her unimpressed, she for the first time came to understand her error in her encounter with Ellison's interview? Knott's essayistic attempt to unravel this gordian knot proceeds in 20 short sections ranging from three to nine pages. Twenty essays to understand a letter of 20 lines. All to try to understand, what it was in Ellison's interview that "gave Arendt to think." (22)

• • •

The Bloomingdale neighborhood where Arendt lived bordered on Harlem and was an intersection of immigrant and Black American culture. Arendt's good friend and unofficial social secretary Charlotte Beradt (author of *The Third Reich of Dreams*) lived nearby, and Beradt, as Jana Schmidt has recently discovered, actively sought out Black American cultural and political experiences. She went to Harlem nightclubs and wrote journalistic reports on Black political life. Shortly after Arendt traveled to Jerusalem to witness the trial of Adolf Eichmann and just a few years before Arendt encountered Ellison's interview, Beradt attended the trial of the Black men accused and falsely convicted of murdering Malcolm X.

Unlike her friend, Arendt steered clear of an engagement in Black cultural and political affairs. She was honored in 1964 alongside Ralph Ellison and James Baldwin, at the American Academy of Arts and Letters, but there is no record in her posthumous papers of this event. There are, writes Knott, "few traces of a dialogue with Black authors or poets contained in her *Nachlass*." (67) Outside of a short letter to James Baldwin—which Knott, not without reason, calls a "patronizing gesture"—the one other letter to a well-known Black American intellectual is the now infamous letter Arendt wrote and possibly sent to Ralph Ellison.

• • •

The question of race has come to the forefront of criticism as it relates to Arendt's work. New books and essays have sought to consider her comments and at times her silences on the history of racism and the violence against the Black person in the United States, as well as her earlier remarks about savage tribes in Africa in *The Origins of Totalitarianism*. Most of these books seek either to condemn or to defend Arendt. Knott has written, instead, a nuanced and powerful essay that aims to understand the German-Jewish-stateless refugee and her lifelong engagement with the question of race, all through the lens of Arendt's short unanswered letter to Ralph Ellison.

The engagement between Arendt and Ellison has inauspicious beginnings. Knott is surprised to find that, "In her library Arendt had, to my astonishment, not one book by Ralph Waldo Ellison." (26) And yet Arendt and Ellison share a deep and connected love for freedom: "Freedom is in Ellison and Arendt the idea, that human action as the power to bend the course of history and thus to ease the burden of the past." (36) There are moments, both thinkers argue, when courage is needed to act—and sometimes not to act. But above all, both "warned independently of each other of the danger or the seduction of conformity, which both, briefly expressed, saw as a kind of complicitous coordination (*Gleichschaltung*)." (37)

So, what is it that upset Ellison in Arendt's text? And what did Arendt find so persuasive in Ellison's critique? One answer is heard in the title of Ellison's interview, "Naked Violence and the Idea of Sacrifice." Arendt wrote in her letter, "It is precisely this 'ideal of sacrifice,' which I didn't understand." But Knott pushes further and notes that "Ellison's rejection of Arendt's standpoint was of a more fundamental nature. . . . He asked in the interview, how it could be, that she shut her eyes before the actual daily emergency and pain not to mention the systematic exclusion of blacks from the formation of the country." (55) Ellison saw that Arendt "had absolutely no conception of the situation of blacks." (55)

As she read the interview, Arendt must have understood the depth of her oversight. Ellison's critique of Arendt concerns not the pain of sacrifice, but rather "a call to realize the true American ideal." (57) For Knott, what Arendt saw in Ellison's letter was a recognition of how fully the racism of the country had betrayed its ideals, and how her embrace of those ideals could not continue in the face of such racism. She saw in Ellison's interview how her imagination of the United States as non-national state where all persons were equally guaranteed the right to act and speak in the public realm was still a violent fiction for Black Americans. She realized, Knott suggests, that the United States "were not the United States Arendt had imagined." (65)

The year Arendt wrote her letter to Ellison was also the height of the Civil Rights Movement in the United States. Arendt suddenly began writing about the question of race in the United States. And she carried over insights from her analysis of antisemitism in Europe to help to make sense of anti-Black racism in the United States. She understood "racism as an instrument for rule." (93) Thus, she distinguished racism from guilt and especially collective guilt. Against collective guilt, Arendt held out the idea of collective responsibility: A promise to make the future reliable and fair for all. It is behind this call for responsibility that Knott traces Arendt's interest in Civil Disobedience to at once shed light on the reality of past slavery and present racial discrimination and aim to build a better world.

And here again, in Arendt's warning against collective white guilt and her call instead for universal responsibility, Knott finds a concurrence between Arendt and Ellison. Both warn that an overattention to race and racial identities can overwhelm true human relations. Each worries that separatism and identity politics will undermine the American ideal of freedom. What Arendt, and also Ellison, ultimately shared was the belief, that "The meaning of politics is not apology, but freedom." (109)

Notes

1. See a reproduction of the letter in Knott, 10.

Contributors

Contributors

James Barry Jr. is emeritus professor of philosophy at Indiana University Southeast and lecturer at the University of Louisville. He is of author of *Measures of Science* (Northwestern University Press) and coeditor of *Merleau-Ponty: Texts and Dialogues* (Humanities Press). He is editor of the journal *Arendt Studies* published by the Philosophy Documentation Center. He is cofounder of the Hannah Arendt Circle. His most recent articles include "The Growth of the Social Realm in Arendt's Post-Mortem of the Modern Nation-State" and "The Risk of Total Divergence: Politicized Intelligence and Defactualization in the Age of Imminent War." He is currently completing two book-length studies, one on the legacies of expropriation and the rise of the state of modern poverty at play in Arendt's work and the other on the ways in which the loss of land-based communities sets the stage for our postindustrial consumeristic world.

Thomas Bartscherer is the Peter Sourian Senior Lecturer in the Humanities at Bard College. Current projects include *When the People Rule: Popular Sovereignty in Theory and Practice* for (coeditor, Cambridge University Press), and the new critical edition of Hannah Arendt's *The Life of the Mind*, forthcoming in the *Complete Works* series. *Stranger Love*, an opera he created with composer Dylan Mattingly, will premiere in 2023. His research and teaching interests include literature and philosophy in antiquity, the reception of ancient motifs in modern and contemporary culture, and the theory and practice of liberal democracy.

Roger Berkowitz has been teaching political theory, legal thought, and human rights at Bard College since 2005. He is the academic director of the Hannah Arendt Center for Politics and Humanities at Bard College. Professor Berkowitz is an interdisciplinary scholar, teacher, and writer. His interests stretch from Greek and German philosophy to legal history and from the history of science to images of justice in film and literature. He is the author of *The Gift of Science: Leibniz and the Modern Legal Tradition*; coeditor of *Thinking in Dark Times: Hannah Arendt on Ethics and Politics*; editor of "Revenge and Justice," a special issue of *Law, Culture, and the Humanities*; and a contributing editor to *Rechtsgeschichte*. His essays have appeared in numerous academic journals. Roger Berkowitz received his BA from Amherst College; JD from Boalt Hall School of Law, University of California, Berkeley; and PhD from UC Berkeley.

Hollie Russon Gilman is a political scientist, lecturer, adviser, and civic strategist working at the intersection of civic engagement, digital technology, and governance. She is currently a senior fellow at New America's Political Reform Program and Visiting Fellow at Harvard's Ash Center for Democratic Governance and Innovation. She is particularly interested in revitalizing American democracy, local innovation, and the opportunities and challenges of digital technologies to enhance governance and improve equity. She holds a PhD and MA from Harvard's Department of Government as well as an AB from the University of Chicago with highest honors in political science. Her first book *Democracy Reinvented: Participatory Budgeting and Civic Innovation in the United States* was noted by Inc.com as a critical book for deciding the future of our cities. Her most recent book *Civic Power: Rebuilding American Democracy in an Era of Democratic Crisis* (2019 with Sabeel Rahman, published by Cambridge University Press), explores how we can empower traditionally marginalized communities and underserved stakeholders to have a greater voice and power in civic life and policy making.

Shmuel Lederman is a research fellow at the Weiss-Livnat Center for Holocaust Research and Education at the University of Haifa, and a lecturer at the University of Haifa and at the Open University of Israel. He also serves as assistant editor of the journal *History & Memory*. His main fields of interest are political theory and genocide studies. He has published numerous articles on Hannah Arendt's political thought, and the book, *Hannah Arendt and Participatory Democracy: A People's Utopia* (published in 2019 by Palgrave Macmillan).

Matthew Longo is assistant professor of political science at Leiden University. He received a PhD from Yale University in 2014 and is the recipient of the Leo Strauss Award for the Best Doctoral Dissertation in Political Philosophy, given by the American Political Science Association (APSA). His first book, *The Politics of Borders: Sovereignty, Security, and the Citizen after 9/11* (published by Cambridge University Press in 2018), won the Charles Taylor Book Award.

Michael K. MacKenzie is assistant professor of political science in the Department of Political Science at the University of Pittsburgh. His research interests include democratic theory, intergenerational relations, deliberation, political representation, institutional design, and public engagement. His book project, *Future Publics: Democracy, Deliberation, and Future-Regarding Action*, is about the challenges and possibilities of making long-term decisions in democratic systems. He holds a PhD in Political Science from the University of British Columbia (2013) and a master's degree in political science and social statistics from McGill University (2006). He was a democracy fellow and post-doctoral researcher at the Ash Center for Democratic Governance and Innovation at the Harvard Kennedy School. In 2006–07 he worked as a policy analyst and facilitator with the Ontario Citizens' Assembly on Electoral Reform and has since helped to run several other randomly selected assemblies, both large and small.

Shaan Sachdev is a cultural critic in New York City. He writes about ontology, political bias, the military-industrial complex, queer city life, and his two favorite divas: Hannah Arendt and Beyoncé. He graduated from Bard in 2011. His essays have also appeared in *The Point*, *The New Republic*, *Slate*, and the *Los Angeles Review of Books*.

Yasemine Sari is assistant professor of philosophy in the Department of Philosophy and World Religions at the University of Northern Iowa. As a political philosopher, her work mainly focuses on democratic political theory, especially as it relates to human rights, extrainstitutional recognition, and the borders between citizen and noncitizen. Her current research takes up the global refugee crisis.

Allison Stanger is the Russell Leng '60 Professor of International Politics and Economics at Middlebury College, Technology and Human Values Senior Fellow at Harvard University's Edmund J. Safra Center for Ethics, New America Cybersecurity Fellow, and an external professor at the Santa Fe Institute. She is the author of *Whistleblowers: Honesty in America from Washington to Trump* and *One Nation Under Contract: The Outsourcing of American Power and the Future of Foreign Policy* (Yale University Press). She is working on a new book tentatively titled *Consumers vs. Citizens: Social Inequality and Democracy's Public Square in a Big Data World*. Stanger's writing has appeared in *Foreign Affairs*, *Foreign Policy*, *Financial Times*, *International Herald Tribune*, *New York Times*, *USA Today*, and the *Washington Post*, and she has testified before the Commission on Wartime Contracting, the Senate Budget Committee, the Congressional Oversight Panel, the Senate HELP Committee, and the House Committee on Government Oversight and Reform. She is a member of the Council on Foreign Relations and received her PhD in political science from Harvard University. In 2021, Stanger was named senior advisor of the Hannah Arendt Humanities Network.

Tracy B. Strong (1943–2022) was professor of political theory and philosophy at the University of Southampton (United Kingdom) and UCSD Distinguished Professor, emeritus. He authored many articles and several books, most recently *Politics without Vision:'Thinking without a Banister' in the Twentieth Century* (Chicago) and *'Learning our Native Tongue':Citizenship, Contestation and Conflict in America* (Chicago). From 1990 until 2000, he was editor of *Political Theory. An International Journal of Political Philosophy*. He was recently exploring and publishing on the political thought of the great writers of the 19th-century American Renaissance.

David Van Reybrouck recently published the bestseller *Revolusi: Indonesia and the Birth of the Modern World*. Van Reybrouck is considered "one of the leading intellectuals in Europe" (*Der Tagesspiegel*), and is a pioneering advocate of participatory democracy. He founded the G1000 Citizens' Summit, and his work has led to trials in participatory democracy throughout Europe. He is also one of the most highly regarded literary and political writers of his generation. His book *Congo: The Epic History of a People*, won 19 prizes, sold 500,000 copies, and has been translated into a dozen languages. It was described as a "masterpiece" by the *Independent* and "magnificent" by the *New York Times*. His essay "Against Elections: The Case for Democracy" was translated into more than 20 languages and was praised by Kofi Annan.

About Bard College

Founded in 1860, Bard College in Annandale-on-Hudson, New York, is an independent, residential, coeducational college offering a four-year BA program in the liberal arts and sciences and a five-year BA/BS degree in economics and finance. The Bard College Conservatory of Music offers a five-year program in which students pursue a dual degree—a BM and a BA in a field other than music. Bard offers MM degrees in conjunction with the Conservatory and The Orchestra Now, and MM as well as MM in music education at Longy School of Music of Bard College in Cambridge, Massachusetts. Bard and its affiliated institutions also grant the following degrees: AA at the Bard Early Colleges, public schools with campuses in New York City, Baltimore, Cleveland, New Orleans, Washington, DC, and Newark, New Jersey, and at three Bard Microcolleges; AA and BA at Bard College at Simon's Rock in Great Barrington, Massachusetts, and through the Bard Prison Initiative at six correctional institutions in New York State; MA in curatorial studies, MS and MA in economic theory and policy, MEd in environmental education; MS in environmental policy and in climate science and policy; MAT; and MA in human rights and the arts at the Annandale campus; MFA at multiple campuses; MBA in sustainability in New York City; MA in global studies in Vienna and New York City; and MA, MPhil, and PhD in the decorative arts, design history, and material culture at the Bard Graduate Center in Manhattan. Internationally, Bard confers BA and MAT degrees at Al-Quds University in East Jerusalem and American University of Central Asia in Kyrgyzstan; and BA degrees at Bard College Berlin: A Liberal Arts University.

Bard offers nearly 50 academic programs in four divisions and interdivisional disciplines. Total enrollment for Bard College and its affiliates is approximately 6,000 students. The undergraduate College has an enrollment of about 1,800 and a student-to-faculty ratio of 10:1. Bard's acquisition of the Montgomery Place estate has brought the size of the campus to nearly 1,000 acres. For more information about Bard College, visit bard.edu.

JOURNALS

Made in USA - North Chelmsford, MA
1321667_9781936192748
07.13.2022 0952